STUDIES IN THE TEACHING
OF OUR LORD

Studies in the Teaching of Our Lord

BY

HENRY BARCLAY SWETE, D.D., Litt.D.

REGIUS PROFESSOR OF DIVINITY IN THE UNIVERSITY
OF CAMBRIDGE

εἷς γάρ ἐστιν ὑμῶν ὁ διδάσκαλος

SECOND EDITION

WIPF & STOCK · Eugene, Oregon

To

E. J. S.

Wipf and Stock Publishers
199 W 8th Ave, Suite 3
Eugene, OR 97401

Studies in the Teaching of Our Lord
By Swete, Henry Barclay
ISBN 13: 978-1-55635-751-0
ISBN 10: 1-55635-751-6
Publication date 12/3/2007
Previously published by Hodder and Stoughton, 1904

THE following Studies have been reprinted with a few changes, chiefly verbal, from the *Expositor* for 1903.

They touch but the fringe of a great subject which has often been treated at length, but it is hoped that their brevity may appeal to some who have no leisure for longer works.

The aim of the writer will be attained if any reader is led by these chapters to examine with greater interest the Master's words as they are reported in the Four Gospels.

CONTENTS

CHAPTER I

PAGE

THE CONDITIONS AND GENERAL CHARACTER OF THE TEACHING 11

CHAPTER II

THE TEACHING IN THE MARCAN TRADITION . 39

CHAPTER III

THE NON-MARCAN TEACHING IN ST. MATTHEW . 67

CHAPTER IV

THE TEACHING PECULIAR TO ST. LUKE . . 97

CHAPTER V

THE TEACHING IN THE GOSPEL OF ST. JOHN . 127

CHAPTER VI

THE TEACHING CONSIDERED AS A WHOLE . 159

THE CONDITIONS AND GENERAL
CHARACTER OF THE TEACHING

CHAPTER I

THE CONDITIONS AND GENERAL CHARACTER OF THE TEACHING

IT is one of the merits of early Christian theology that it lays frequent emphasis upon the claim of Jesus Christ to be the supreme Teacher of men. This claim is based partly upon the relation which He bears to the world as the Eternal Word, partly upon the recorded teaching of the Ministry. "There is one Teacher," Ignatius writes, "who spake and it was done. He who truly possesses the word of Jesus can learn even from His silence. We endure, in order that we may be found disciples of Jesus Christ, our only Teacher; how can we live apart from Him? Even the prophets were His disciples through the Spirit, and looked for Him as their Teacher."[1] "The utterances that fell from Him," Justin explains, "were brief and concise, for He was no sophist, but His word was the power of God."[2] "Who that has been rightly instructed and has become a friend of the Word," asks an early Alexandrian writer, "does not seek to have a clear understanding of the lessons which were openly taught by the Word to His disciples?"[3] With Clement of Alexandria the thought of Christ the Teacher becomes an inspiration. "Our Tutor," he exclaims, "is the holy and Divine Jesus, the Word who is the Guide of all humanity. The Christian life in which we are now receiving our education is an ordered succession of reasonable actions, an unbroken fulfilment of the teaching of the Word. He is the Teacher who educates the ripe scholar by mysteries, the ordinary believer by hopes of a better life, the hardened through corrective discipline operating upon the senses."[4]

[1] Ign. *Eph.* 15, *Magn.* 9.
[2] Just. *Apol.* i. 14.
[3] *Ep. ad Diog.* 11.
[4] Clem. Al. *Paed.* i. 7. 55, 13. 102 ; *Strom.* vii. 2. 6.

In the present series of studies we shall take a narrower view of the teaching of Christ than that which forms the theme of Clement's great work. We shall confine ourselves to the teaching recorded in the Four Gospels. The Ministry was a particular manifestation of the didactic energy of the Word, a manifestation limited both in scope and in duration. But its very limitations may attract some who are not prepared to commit themselves to the guidance of the Christian mystic. The Gospels reveal our Lord as exercising the office of Teacher under the conditions of human life, and they place the teaching in relation with human history. It is with this tangible evidence of Christ's power as a Teacher that the study of His didactic work will naturally begin.

This chapter must be devoted to a sketch of the conditions under which our Lord taught, and the chief features which characterized His teaching.

1. In the Palestine of the first century there was no lack of religious teaching. The scribe

was a familiar figure in Galilee as well as in Judæa; he was to be met everywhere—in the synagogue, in the market-place, in the houses of the rich. With him went a numerous following of attached scholars. The first business of the Rabbi was to "raise up many disciples," and the first care of the good Jew to "make to himself a master."[1] It is not without a bitter reminiscence of the religious condition of Palestine that St. James of Jerusalem counsels the members of the Christian communities to which he wrote, "Be not many teachers, my brethren, knowing that we shall receive heavier judgment."[2] In Christ's day, however, few appear to have questioned the sincerity or the competency of a Rabbi. Wherever he went he was treated with respect; in places of public resort he received the greetings of all who recognised him; in the synagogue he sat on the front benches, and at banquets was among the most honoured guests.[3]

[1] *Pirqe Aboth*, i. 1, 17.
[2] James iii. 1.
[3] Matt. xxiii. 6 f.

ITS GENERAL CHARACTER

As soon as a band of personal followers began to gather round the Lord, He was addressed as "Rabbi," not only by His disciples [1] but generally.[2] The title seems not to have been restricted to Scribes; [3] in popular use it denoted only that the person so accosted claimed to be a public teacher of religion. In this sense Christ accepted the designation.[4] That He did so is the more significant, because He strictly forbade His disciples to assume it.[5] In the Christian Society His position as "the Teacher" was to be unique. He did not, like the Scribes, aim at creating a school of teachers. The Apostolic Church, indeed, possessed an order of "teachers," which was of Divine appointment; [6] but the spirit of Christ's prohibition is to be heard in more than one passage in the Epistles.[7] The

---

[1] John i. 38; Mark ix. 5.
[2] Mark v. 35; x. 17, 51.
[3] It is given to the Baptist (John iii. 26).
[4] Mark xiv. 14; John xiii. 13 f.
[5] Matt. xxiii. 8 f.
[6] 1 Cor. xii. 28, οὓς μὲν ἔθετο ὁ θεὸς ἐν τῇ ἐκκλησίᾳ . . . τρίτον διδασκάλους.
[7] 1 Thess. iv. 9. 1 John ii. 27.

saying: "One is your teacher, and ye all are brethren," was of permanent import in so far as it asserted the supremacy of the Master, and the substantial equality of all His disciples in their relation to Him.

2. That Jesus took rank among the Rabbis did not conceal but rather accentuated the difference which separated the Prophet of Nazareth from the other religious teachers of the time. Men could not but institute a comparison between the new Rabbi and the teachers to whom they had so long been accustomed. The latter were moulded after one pattern; they had been produced by the same process, they followed the same methods, and taught on the whole the same doctrines. Each of them had himself been the disciple of a Rabbi, "brought up at the feet" of one who had "received" from his predecessor. The teaching was traditional; if from time to time new features were added, they were on the lines of earlier decisions, or differed from them only by entering into minuter details. In all these respects the contrast presented by the new Teacher was complete. The home life

at Nazareth had supplied His only preparation for the teacher's office; if He had acquired the elements of learning from the master of the synagogue school, with the higher education imparted by the Scribes He had no acquaintance;[1] in the place of professional training He could produce nothing but the experience gained in an obscure village and varied only by an occasional visit to Jerusalem, or such knowledge as could be gathered from observation and from a study of the Law, the Psalms, and the Prophets. Nor was His method of teaching less singular than His training for the teacher's office. The common people, no bad judges of distinctions which depend upon character and personality, recognised in it something which was wholly new. "They were greatly struck at His teaching," St. Mark forcibly observes, "for He taught them as one having authority, and not after the manner of the Scribes."[2] This remark is placed by St. Matthew at the end of the Sermon on the Mount,[3] but in St. Mark it holds what is

[1] John vii. 15; πῶς οὗτος γράμματα οἶδεν μὴ μεμαθηκώς;
[2] Mark i. 22.   [3] Matt. vii. 28 f.

doubtless its original place, coming immediately after the first Sabbath discourse in the synagogue at Capernaum. One address in the synagogue was enough to convince an untrained but devout audience that this was no Rabbi of the ordinary type. The distinguishing note of His teaching was "authority" (ἐξουσία), not so much unusual capacity as the consciousness of a Divine right to teach; not learning, but the force of truth. Here was a Teacher who had no need to appeal to older authorities, but stood upon His own right. The discourse was no doubt based upon the usual lesson from the Law or the Prophets, but the interpretation rested simply on the testimony of the speaker. He seemed to speak that which He knew, and to bear witness of that which He had seen.[1] No great Rabbi was quoted in support of what He said; it carried conviction by the simple weight of an αὐτὸς ἔφα. Yet He who spake was a man of thirty, and it was the first time, at least in Capernaum, that He had used His privilege of addressing His brother Israelites. The

[1] John iii. 11.

ITS GENERAL CHARACTER

authority which held the audience spell-bound was not the magic of a great reputation, but the irresistible force of a Divine message, delivered under the sense of a Divine mission. Nothing could have been more opposed to the traditionalism of the Scribes, who did not venture a step beyond the beaten path, and even there leaned heavily upon the authority of their predecessors.

3. It was a "new teaching" [1] which was heard that Sabbath day in the synagogue of Capernaum, and its freshness was not limited to method. Our Lord's teaching was not indeed "original," in the sense of being the outcome of human genius. He distinctly disclaimed originality of this kind: "My teaching," He said, "is not Mine, but His that sent Me." [2] Moreover, its novelty was not absolute but relative. It came as a surprise to those whose circle of religious ideas had from childhood been filled by the jargon of the Scribes, and the party cries of contemporary Judaism. Jesus was not a disciple of Hillel or of Shammai;

[1] Mark i. 27, τί ἐστιν τοῦτο; διδαχὴ καινή.
[2] John v 16.

He was neither Pharisee nor Sadducee nor Essene; His sympathies were not with Nationalists, Herodians, or Hellenists. The one topic which seemed to possess His mind and overflowed into His teaching was the Kingdom of God. But in this there was nothing essentially new; it was in its central thought as old as the Law and the Prophets; it had kindled the fire of devotion which burns in many of the Psalms. The Lord did not come to revolutionize the faith of Israel, as some soon began to suspect; His antagonism to the teaching of the Scribes and Pharisees was not due to any secret design against the national religion. "Think not," He explained, "that I came to destroy the Law or the Prophets; I came not to destroy, but to fulfil."[1] His teaching had its roots in the teaching of the Old Testament; it merely brought the latter to its legitimate and appointed end. He was in the direct line of succession from Moses and Elijah; in Him they found their consummation, the goal to which they had half unconsciously been reaching forth, the Teacher

[1] Matt. v. 17.

ITS GENERAL CHARACTER 21

whose voice revived and perfected their fragmentary expositions of the truth.[1] It was His mission to give effect to ideals which had long floated before the imagination of the Covenant people. Thus the teaching of the great Scribe of the Kingdom of Heaven was old even while it was new,[2] carrying the old further, but never breaking from it; fulfilling and not destroying it, but rather bearing it on to its completion and accomplishment.[3]

4. The Kingdom of God or of Heaven—the terms are practically synonymous [4] — covers more adequately than any other single phrase the whole field of our Lord's teaching. His Gospel was "the Gospel of the Kingdom"; [5] it brought the good news that the reign of God on earth was about to begin. The conception of the Divine sovereignty lay at the root of the theocratic constitution of Israel; it inspired

[1] Cf. Matt. xvii. 3–5; Heb. i. 1 f.
[2] Cf. Matt. xiii. 52.
[3] Cf. (but in reference to another sphere of Christ's activity) Heb. i. 3, φέρων τε τὰ πάντα, with Westcott's note *ad loc.*
[4] See Dalman, *Worte Jesu*, i. p. 75 ff.
[5] Matt. iii. 2.

the Messianic hope; it colours the splendid visions of the Prophets. Yet both in the announcement of the immediate approach of the Divine Kingdom, and the interpretation which was given to the Kingdom, Jesus struck a note which had not been sounded before. According to St. Matthew, indeed, the Baptist had already proclaimed that the Kingdom was at hand; but St. Mark attributes the words to our Lord,[1] and neither St. Mark nor St. Luke recognises an earlier use of them by the Forerunner. Certainly it was in Christ's teaching that the idea took shape and became a permanent factor in religious thought. As for the interpretation of the Kingdom, it is no exaggeration to say that this forms the staple of the instructions which our Lord gave to His Galilean hearers. It was here that He departed most widely from prevalent beliefs, and may indeed have seemed to many to depart from the teaching of the Prophets. The Prophets had drawn a glowing picture of the glories of the Messianic Kingdom, and in the pre-Christian

[1] Mark i. 15. So also does St. Matthew a little further on (iv. 17).

ITS GENERAL CHARACTER 23

apocalyptic writings a vast eschatology had grown up around the earlier hope. But in our Lord's presentation of the Kingdom eschatology falls into the background, while even the prophetic picture loses much of its colouring. The parables may be taken to exhibit the sovereignty of God in the light in which Christ meant it to appear before the people. They compare it to the sowing, growth, and harvesting of the crops; to the labours of the merchant, the fisherman, the housewife;[1] to the relations of the master of a great house with the members of his household;[2] to a marriage feast and incidents connected with it.[3] These homely illustrations bring the Kingdom into the heart of ordinary life, not only by appealing to common experience, but by representing the Divine Rule as a force working within men, and not merely controlling them from without. The same conception is to be noticed in sayings of our Lord which are not cast in a parabolic form. The Kingdom of God belongs to

[1] Matt. xiii. 1 ff., Mark iv. 1 ff.
[2] Matt. xxv. 14 ff., Luke xix. 11 f.
[3] Matt. xxii. 2 ff., xxv. 1 ff.; Mark ii. 19.

the poor in spirit, to those who are persecuted for righteousness' sake;[1] the position which men will hold in it depends on their moral character;[2] the rich and great of this world enter it with difficulty;[3] it comes not "with observation," so that men can say of it "Lo here" or "Lo there," but is to be sought around us or within;[4] it cannot be entered, it cannot be seen, except by those who have been born into a new order and possess spiritual faculties.[5] The Kingdom of God is coupled with the righteousness of God;[6] it is the great moral and spiritual lever which is designed to lift men's lives up to the Divine standards of goodness and truth.

If this teaching was novel, it must have been to many disappointing in the extreme. Notwithstanding the popular form in which it was expressed, there was nothing in it which pandered to the popular taste. It took no account of the national expectations of restored independence and an imperial mission. It

---

[1] Matt. v. 3, 10.
[2] *Ibid.* 19.
[3] Mark x. 23 f.
[4] Luke xvii. 20 f.
[5] John iii. 3, 5.
[6] Matt. vi. 33.

offered no worldly advantages; it discouraged the vicious passions of men; it limited itself strictly to the ethical and spiritual. Yet the preaching of the Kingdom, as Christ preached it, fascinated thousands of the common people. There was in it that which touched the springs of human life; those who heard it knew themselves to be face to face with ultimate realities. And there was in the Teacher that which corresponded with the teaching; no suspicion of insincerity, no hardness of professional formalism, no flourish of ambitious rhetoric, no self-seeking or display spoiled its general effect. Every word rang true and went home. Morality as taught by Christ was neither dull commonplace nor arid philosophy, but a matter of vital interest; the spiritual order, as He revealed it, was seen to environ the life of man; the powers of the world to come were upon His hearers,[1] and they seemed to be standing in the presence of God. No wonder that " the people all hung upon Him, listening."[2]

[1] Cf. what is said (though in another connexion) in Matt. xii. 28, ἔφθασεν ἐφ' ὑμᾶς ἡ βασιλεία τοῦ θεοῦ.

[2] Luke xix. 48.

But the enthusiasm evoked by His teaching was not to be limited to a single generation. The teaching asserted principles of universal application, and it clothed them in the plain strong language which is the best vehicle of religious truth. The Lord knew that in addressing the peasants of Galilee He was speaking to the world. This Gospel of the Kingdom must be preached to all nations, and with it would be spread the knowledge of even the smallest incidents connected with His ministry.[1] History has more than verified His prediction; written Gospels stand behind the preached Gospel, and enshrine in immortal pages the sayings of Jesus Christ. Teaching such as His could not die; its permanence was guaranteed not only by its Divine origin, but by its correspondence with the deepest needs of men, and its clear unfaltering statement of those eternal truths to which the human conscience pays homage even when the will does not render a prompt obedience.

5. There is another element in our Lord's teaching which is specially prominent in the

[1] Matt. xxiv. 14, xxvi. 13.

ITS GENERAL CHARACTER 27

Fourth Gospel, though it is not altogether overlooked by the Synoptists. Jesus not only proclaimed the Gospel of the Kingdom, but He proclaimed Himself as standing in a unique relation both to God and to men. In the Synoptic teaching, *i.e.*, the teaching in Galilee, this relation is usually kept in the background of the thought; He is content to speak of Himself as the "Son of man";[1] but occasionally He permits Himself to be called "the Son of God,"[2] and even calls God His Father in a sense which implies a peculiar sonship.[3] In the Johannine teaching, especially in that part of it which belongs to Jerusalem,[4] His relation to the Father is handled with much fulness, and on many occasions both public and private. We need not stop here to inquire into the import of this Christology; it is enough to note that it has a place in all the records of Christ's teaching, although not the same place. In Galilee His first purpose was to

---

[1] *E.g.*, Matt. xi. 19.
[2] *E.g.*, Mark v. 7; Matt. xiv. 33, xvi. 16.
[3] Matt. xi. 25 ff., xii. 50, xv. 13.
[4] See cc. v., viii., x., xiv.–xvii.

awaken the consciences of the multitudes who were indifferent to the realities of the spiritual Kingdom, and the message rather than the person of the Messenger occupied His thoughts and filled His instructions. But in Jerusalem, among the learned, and on the historic ground of the Temple courts, He did not shrink from answering the questions which were rising in men's minds about Himself. There is no cause for suspecting the genuineness of the discourses in the Fourth Gospel which deal with this subject; such a passage as Matthew xi. 25–30 shews that the elements of the Johannine Christology were present in the mind of our Lord during His ministry in Galilee, although the conditions which surrounded Him there did not call for frequent or detailed reference to it. Sooner or later the self-revelation could not but have been made. The Teacher of the Church is inseparable from His teaching; the Gospel of the Kingdom is also "the Gospel of Jesus Christ the Son of God,"[1] and no

---

[1] Mark i. 1. Υἱοῦ θεοῦ, if not part of the original title of St. Mark, at least sums up the impression derived from the reading of the "earliest Gospel."

presentation of it is complete which leaves out of sight His Person and relation to the Father. A Christianity without a Christology is no true description of the Gospel as Christ taught it at Jerusalem or even at Capernaum.

6. Both in Jerusalem and in Galilee our Lord's teaching was partly delivered in public, partly addressed in private to His disciples. The distinction is not unimportant, for the private teaching differed from the public both in aim and methods.

The Lord began with the people at large, addressing Himself to the pious who attended the synagogues, and to the mixed crowds who gathered round Him on the shore of the lake or by the roadside. His message was to all, and He devoted His first and, to the end, His chief attention to the outside crowd. There is in His public teaching no trace of contempt for the *'am haaretz*,[1] no lofty superciliousness; their ignorance awakened no impatience in Him, but

[1] Contrast John vii. 49, and Hillel's caustic saying in *Aboth* ii. 6, ed. Taylor: "He used to say, 'No boor is a sin-fearer, nor is the vulgar pious.'"

30 TEACHING OF OUR LORD

only an infinite compassion which impelled Him to give them of His best.[1] But from the first an inner circle of disciples claimed His special attention. St. John enables us to see how this "little flock" had its beginnings. One or two of the disciples of the Baptist found themselves drawn to the new Teacher, followed Him to His lodging, spent the night in His company, and in the end resolved to share His life. The number might have become inconveniently large, had not Jesus Himself reduced it to twelve.[2] These select disciples received special instructions, chiefly when the hours of public instruction were over. He explained to them the teaching which had been given in parables to "those outside";[3] He entrusted to them "the secret of the Kingdom of God."[4] Yet they were warned at the time that they received this additional teaching in trust for the whole Church; it was imparted to them only that they might be prepared, when the right moment came, to deliver it to the world. It was not an esoteric teaching in the strictest

[1] Matt. ix. 36 f.
[2] Mark iii. 13 f.
[3] Mark iv. 10 f., 34.
[4] *Ibid.* 11.

sense, not the heritage of a privileged order, but the common property of the Christian Society, spoken for the moment into the ear, but one day to be proclaimed upon the housetops.[1] The line which the Master drew between His two methods of teaching was temporary and not permanent, due to circumstances and not to any essential difference.

7. What effect Christ's teaching has had upon the world we know. But it is natural to ask how far it impressed those who were brought directly under its influence. It is strange to find but one reference in the Acts to Christian communities in Galilee;[2] it would seem as if little permanent impression had been produced, and we know from our Lord's own words that the chief lake-side towns in which He preached were unmoved at the time.[3] But the crowds which attended His preaching in Galilee were not all Galileans; Judæa, Idumæa, Peræa, and even Phœnicia were represented, whilst the great roads which crossed Galilee in all directions carried His fame through Syria.[4] It

[1] Matt. x. 27.
[2] Acts ix. 31.
[3] Matt. xi. 20 ff.
[4] Matt. iv. 23; Mark iii. 7f.

is impossible to determine how far the early spread of the Palestinian Church was due to these influences, to say nothing of effects produced upon individual lives, or of the priceless treasure which the Church has inherited in the records of the Galilean ministry.

Nor is it less difficult to arrive at a clear estimate of the effects of Christ's teaching of the Twelve. The results, so far as they can be discovered by a casual reading of the evidence, seem to be sadly disproportionate to the time and labour bestowed. The Apostles do not upon the whole appear to have been men remarkable either for beauty or strength of character, or for judgement, insight, or breadth of view. If we put out of sight the apocryphal Acts, only two out of the Twelve have left any appreciable mark upon Christendom. But the influence exerted by a college of trained men cannot be estimated simply by the recorded work of the individuals who composed it. The Apostolic body formed, as the Acts of the Apostles shew, a nucleus which gave coherence and order to the nascent Church; in it the Church found a centre of unity; from it she

ITS GENERAL CHARACTER 33

received initiation and guidance in new movements, and a standard of teaching which was never wholly lost.[1] As soon as the Palestinian Church, the mother of a future Christendom, was able to stand alone, the Apostles were scattered, and their corporate action ceased. But even if St. Peter had not laboured both in East and West, or St. John at Ephesus, the years of patient training which the Apostles received in Galilee would not have been fruitless. The Great Teacher had in this way safeguarded the infancy of the Church, and created a deposit of doctrine and a basis of order which are with us to this day.

If we may accept the witness of the Fourth Gospel, the Master did not regard His work of teaching as ended by His death. "I have yet many things to say unto you," He declared on the night before the Passion, "but ye cannot bear them now; howbeit when He, the Spirit of truth, is come, He shall guide you into all the truth, for He shall not speak from Himself. . . .

---

[1] Acts ii. 42, v. 12 ff., vi. 2; cf. Eph. ii. 20; 2 Pet. iii. 2; Apoc. xxi. 14.

These things have I spoken unto you in proverbs; the hour cometh when I shall no more speak unto you in proverbs, but shall tell you plainly of the Father."[1] The fulfilment of the last words must be sought in the dispensation of the Spirit, who is the Spirit of Jesus[2] and of Christ,[3] sent in the Master's name[4] to speak as His Vicar to the Churches.[5] The teaching of the Spirit, both in the Apostolic Epistles and in the experience of Christendom, is thus a true continuation of the teaching of Christ. The Master, who of old taught in proverbs, teaches now with plainness of speech. To His progressive enlightenment of the Christian consciousness we look with confidence for an answer to the questions which are pressed upon us by the growth of knowledge and the complications of modern life. The Spirit of Christ will bring to the remembrance of the

---

[1] John xvi. 12 f., 25.   [2] Acts xvi. 7.
[3] Rom. viii. 9.   [4] John xiv. 26.
[5] Apoc. ii. 7; cf. Tert. *de praescr.* 13 creditur . . Iesum Christum . . . misisse vicariam vim Spiritus Sancti.

ITS GENERAL CHARACTER 35

Church all that Christ said;[1] He will take of Christ's, and declare it unto her,[2] and in the teaching of Christ, interpreted by the Spirit, will be found in due time the solution of problems which for the moment threaten the foundations of our faith.

[1] John xiv. 26.   [2] John xvi. 14 f.

THE TEACHING IN THE MARCAN
TRADITION

CHAPTER II

THE TEACHING IN THE MARCAN TRADITION

WHEN we proceed to examine our Lord's teaching in detail, it becomes evident that there is more than one way by which the subject may be approached. The Gospels may be taken in the common order, and the testimony of each discussed in turn, as was done by Rudolf Stier sixty years ago. Or we may follow Wendt in his endeavour to reconstruct the teaching on a basis which will represent it in the light of an organic unity. In the present sketches we propose to employ a method which is perhaps better adapted to a brief treatment. We shall interrogate each of the chief sources used by the Evangelists, and when this has been done we shall endeavour to compare and co-ordinate the results.

We begin with the tradition which forms the substance of our earliest Gospel, the Gospel according to St. Mark, and the basis of a large portion of the other Synoptic narratives.

The Marcan tradition has preserved no great discourse and few important parables. Frequent reference is made to the preaching and teaching of Jesus,[1] but His recorded sayings are chiefly incidental remarks or short instructions; the only considerable fragments are the parables of the Sower (iv. 3-9) and the Husbandman (xii. 1-11), and the apocalypse in chapter xiii. This comparative scarcity of recollections of the Lord's teaching is consistent with the statement of Irenæus that St. Mark reproduced the preaching of St. Peter.[2] The primitive preacher would doubtless limit himself to anecdotes and brief sayings, leaving to the catechist the transmission of the Master's discourses.

But the records of Christ's teaching which are to be found in the "memoirs of Peter" are not

---

[1] Mark i. 14, 21 f., 38; ii. 13; iv. 1, 33; vi. 2, 6: vii. 14; xi. 18; xii. 1, 35, 38.

[2] Iren. iii. 1, Μᾶρκος . . . τὰ ὑπὸ Πέτρου κηρυσσόμενα ἐγγράφως ἡμῖν παραδέδωκε.

the less valuable because they are scanty and short. Doubtless the Apostle selected for preaching the sayings which had made the deepest impression upon his memory, or which he judged to be the most characteristic or important. It may prove that the Marcan tradition is thoroughly representative of the teaching as a whole, so that if we have grasped its significance, we possess a key to the understanding of the fuller reports preserved in the other sources.

1. This view is confirmed by the first words attributed to Jesus in the Second Gospel.[1] They are evidently the text, so to speak, of His Galilean preaching; they recite in the most compressed form both its message and its call. "The time is fulfilled, and the Kingdom of God is at hand," is the substance of the Gospel which Christ preached; "repent ye, and believe in the Gospel," is the twofold call which He based upon His announcement. Both message and call were heard during the ministry not once or twice only, but again and again; though clothed in many different forms and presented in vary-

[1] Mark i. 15.

ing degrees of completeness, these topics were never far from the Master's thoughts, and appear in the background if not in the forefront of all His utterances.[1]

2. When the Kingdom of God, the Divine sovereignty over the whole life of man upon earth, presented itself in the person and ministry of Christ, it was confronted by tremendous obstacles. The first and chief of these was human sin, and it is to this that our Lord addresses Himself in the next word which the Marcan tradition ascribes to Him.[2] His remark to the Scribes at Capernaum, "The Son of Man hath authority to forgive sins upon the earth," revealed at the very outset of His work the power by which He intended to fight this enemy. He would do it by proclaiming an ἄφεσις,[3] a full discharge of the sins contracted by men in the past, a discharge which would leave them free to begin their lives afresh. Even the Scribes recognised that God could

---

[1] When, *e.g.*, St. Luke adds εἰς μετάνοιαν to the saying of Mark ii. 17, he merely brings out what was latent in καλέσαι ἁμαρτωλούς.

[2] Mark ii. 10.   [3] Cf. Luke iv. 18 (Isa. lxi. 1).

forgive sins, but the difference is immense between a forgiveness locked up in the treasures of the Divine clemency and a forgiveness committed to man on earth for the benefit of men. The charter of the Kingdom of God opens with the gospel of a present forgiveness. The Scribes rightly judged this claim to be of the first magnitude,[1] nor was it made by Jesus in any spirit of light-hearted optimism, but with a full sense of its significance. That He realized the deep-seated strength of the disease which He undertook to heal is evident from His later saying, "From within, out of the heart of men, evil thoughts proceed."[2] Sin is not, according to Christ, a superficial evil, but one which is both immanent and inveterate; yet, knowing this, He claims the power to set the sinner free from it. Miracles of physical healing were indeed easy when compared with the moral force exerted in an act of absolution; when Jesus said, "Thy sins be forgiven thee," He uttered a harder word than when He bade Lazarus "come forth." But He was conscious of the right to say this harder word, and He

---

[1] Mark ii. 7   [2] Mark vii. 21 ff.

said it at the earliest opportunity; that such a power should be possessed and exerted on earth was the first condition of the Divine Kingdom being set up among men.

3. Other hindrances stood in the way of the Kingdom of God, and they were met with equal determination. Foremost among these was Pharisaic Judaism, with its insistence on external duties and its neglect of "the weightier matters of the Law." The resistance offered to the Gospel by this system is seen in the Marcan tradition in connexion with three questions: the question of weekly fasting,[1] the question of the Sabbath,[2] and the question of using certain forms of ceremonial purification.[3] The first and the third of these observances rested simply upon the tradition of the Rabbis, and our Lord declined to be bound by them in any way; the second, which was required by the Torah, He accepted, but lifted it up to a level high above that which it occupied in the teaching of the Scribes. "The Sabbath was made for man, and not man for the Sabbath,"[4] asserts a

---

[1] Mark ii. 18 ff. [2] Mark ii. 27 f., iii. 4.
[3] Mark vii. 5 ff. [4] Mark ii. 27.

principle which places that institution in the light of a Divine gift, whereas to the Scribes it wore the aspect of an arbitrary law. But in proclaiming the Sabbath to be a gift of the Divine love, Christ left no opening for licence; the inference[1] which He drew was not that every Israelite was free to observe or to neglect it as he pleased, but that the Son of Man had power to regulate its use.[2] With the weekly fasts and "the Jews' manner of purifying"[3] He dealt in a different way. Fasting was not prescribed by the law except on the Day of Atonement, and the fasts observed on Mondays and Thursdays[4] were mischievous if they ministered to ostentation[5] or were imposed on men's consciences as a religious duty. Moreover, to the disciples of Jesus, who were now rejoicing in the light of the Bridegroom's presence, they would have been a burdensome unreality. He had not come to patch the threadbare

[1] Mark ii. 28 (ὥστε).

[2] Compare the anecdote preserved in Cod. D at Luke vi. 5: τῇ αὐτῇ ἡμέρᾳ θεασάμενός τινα ἐργαζόμενον τῷ σαββάτῳ εἶπεν αὐτῷ, Ἄνθρωπε, εἰ μὲν οἶδας τί ποιεῖς μακάριος εἶ· εἰ δὲ μὴ οἶδας, ἐπικατάρατος καὶ παραβάτης εἶ τοῦ νόμου.

[3] John ii. 6. [4] *Didache*, 8. [5] Luke xviii. 12.

cloak of Judaism, or to pour a new spirit into its obsolete practices.[1] Of the ceremonial of purification prescribed by the Rabbis Jesus was even less tolerant. Not only was it purely traditional, as the Scribes confessed,[2] but it encouraged an externalism which was fatal to any sense of the inwardness of the religious life, and opposed to the first principles of the Kingdom of God. Nor was the danger limited, or likely to yield to better teaching. The system worked like leaven,[3] spreading through Jewish society, and it could only be checked by the most rigorous condemnation.

The Gospel of the Kingdom encountered another and more mysterious obstacle. Whatever view may be taken of "possession," it is clear that our Lord is represented in the Marcan tradition as recognising and withstanding an evil power which was more than human. The reality of this power seems to be assumed in His reply to the Scribes from Jerusalem who charged Him with collusion with "Beelzebub." He gave them to understand that He had

[1] Mark ii. 21 f.   [2] Mark vii. 5.
[3] Mark viii. 15 ff.

forced His way into the house of "the Strong," and intended to bind him and spoil his house.[1] In other words, the casting out of the δαιμόνια, however we may interpret this class of miracles, was a symbol of our Lord's purpose to conquer the hostile power which had asserted its claim over human nature, but was in fact foreign to it and could therefore be dispossessed.

4. So far the teaching has been limited to the forces which obstruct or resist the progress of the Kingdom; it now passes to the contents of the conception itself. At this point the Parable comes into use, for the "mystery of the Kingdom,"[2] the secret of its strength and manner of working, could not be imparted to the uninitiated multitude. The Marcan tradition has but three parables at this stage,[3] and they are all based upon the analogy of vegetable growth, which lends itself in an especial manner to the description of spiritual processes. The first parable insists on the importance of character as determining the degree of influence exerted by the Kingdom of God over the

[1] Mark iii. 27. [2] Mark iv. 11.
[3] Mark iv. 3 ff., 26 ff., 31 f.

individual; the second points out the spontaneity and the mystery of spiritual growth; the third foretells the expansion of the small beginnings of the Church into the greatness of a catholic mission. The conversion of the Empire and of the world itself is shadowed forth in the lodging of the birds of heaven under the branches of the tree which had grown from the least of all seeds. Taken together, the three parables cover the whole work of the Christian society in the present world. We see before us in these familiar pictures the entire history of the *Regnum Dei*—its struggle with human indifference, shallowness, and sin; its steady but unobserved assimilation by all who receive it in sincerity; the final triumph of its cause. Every stage in the long record passes under review, from the uncertain start when the birds of the air are ready to devour the seed to the day when they are glad to seek shelter under the cover of the universal Church.

5. A new stage in the teaching is reached when the Galilean ministry is drawing to an end. By this time the Twelve had been brought into the closest association with the

Master. Intimacy had been fostered by two long journeys which they took in His company, the first leading them through Phœnicia to the Decapolis, the second to the sources of the Jordan at the foot of Hermon.[1] These were not preaching-tours, but though they may have been undertaken partly to secure retirement and rest or even personal safety, they were doubtless used as opportunities for the instruction and training of the Apostles. It was at the end of the second of these journeys that our Lord revealed His glory to the innermost circle of the Apostolate in the vision of the Transfiguration. But before He did this, He called forth from Peter a confession of His Messiahship, and then at once proceeded to foretell the Passion. Henceforth the Cross was the keynote of His teaching; He seemed to have found a new text. How it was to be reconciled with the earlier preaching of the Kingdom passed the comprehension of the Twelve. That the "Christ should suffer"[2] was a doctrine altogether foreign to the

[1] Mark vii. 24, 31, viii. 27, ix. 30.
[2] Acts xxvi. 23, εἰ παθητὸς ὁ Χριστός.

Messianic Hope as they had received and entertained it. Repeated predictions, in which the details of the Crucifixion were distinctly foreshadowed,[1] failed to impress them with the certainty of the coming Passion; it loomed before their minds as a disquieting but unimaginable fear.[2] But prediction did not exhaust Christ's teaching of the Cross. The crucifixion of the Master involved the concrucifixion [3] of the disciples, and for this He began at once to prepare them. The first lesson of this kind was shared by the crowd which followed Him through the villages of Cæsarea Philippi; immediately after His rebuke of St. Peter "He called unto Him the multitude with His disciples and said unto them, "If any man is minded (θέλει) to come after Me, let him disown himself (ἀπαρνησάσθω ἑαυτόν), and let him take up his cross and follow Me."[4] "Self-denial," "bearing the cross," have passed

---

[1] Mark viii. 31, ix. 31, x. 33 f.

[2] Mark ix. 32, ἠγνόουν τὸ ῥῆμα.

[3] Rom. vi. 6, ὁ παλαιὸς ἡμῶν ἄνθρωπος συνεσταυρώθη. Gal. ii. 20, Χριστῷ συνεσταύρωμαι.

[4] Mark viii. 34.

amongst Christians into household words, but their true meaning eludes many who use them glibly. The disciple who "denies himself," in the sense intended by Christ, loses himself in the Master, so that, as St. Paul has it, it is no longer he who lives, but Christ who lives in him.[1] The man who takes up his cross not only bears a burden laid upon him, but goes to his death, is prepared to die with Christ, *i.e.*, to pass out of his life of sin into a life unto God.[2] To the crowd the words could have served only as a deterrent, warning off any who took discipleship too lightly; to the Apostles they revealed the true nature of the calling which they had embraced. Henceforth it was the chief concern of the Master to form in these twelve men the type of character which would fit them to deny themselves and take up the cross. We see this in the stern rebuke of personal ambition which followed their return to Capernaum;[3] in the warning that he who would "enter into life" or even escape the

[1] Gal. ii. 20, ζῶ δὲ οὐκέτι ἐγώ, ζῇ δὲ ἐν ἐμοὶ Χριστός.
[2] Rom. vi. 6 ff.; Col. iii. 3.
[3] Mark ix. 33 ff.

"Gehenna of fire" must sacrifice hand or foot or eye when it becomes a stumbling-block;[1] in the intimation that places of honour in the Messianic Kingdom are to be won only by sharing Christ's cup and baptism.[2] The same great lesson is taught when the Master makes childhood the symbol of fitness for the Kingdom,[3] and represents material wealth as a bar to admission which omnipotence only can surmount.[4]

6. Besides self-abnegation Christ impressed upon His followers the necessity of faith. As we have seen, faith was joined with repentance in the original call (i. 15), and it was made the condition of the exercise of our Lord's miraculous powers in the case of rational beings (ii. 5; v. 34, 36; vi. 5 f.; ix. 23; x. 52). On the Twelve it was urged with special earnestness. They had "believed in the Gospel" from the first, but there were moments when their faith seemed to vanish, and the Lord called them back to this primary condition of the Christian

---

[1] Mark ix. 43 ff.
[2] Mark x. 38 f.
[3] Mark x. 14 f., cf. ix. 36 f.
[4] Mark x. 23 ff.

life.[1] But it was especially in connexion with prayer that He enforced the need of faith. The failure of the disciples to cast out an unclean spirit was attributed to the want of prayer,[2] or rather, as St. Matthew states, to the ὀλιγοπιστία which made prayer of no effect. A few days before the end the Lord returned to this matter, ascribing almost boundless powers to prayer inspired by faith: "have faith in God . . . all things whatsoever ye pray and ask for, believe that ye received them (when ye asked), and they shall be yours."[3] He added that mountains might be moved out of their places at the call of an adequate faith. By these words He planted at the centre of man's spiritual life a force of incalculable power; while He took away from His Church the incentive of a self-seeking ambition, He revealed the secret of a strength which could overcome the world.

7. When the scene is shifted from Galilee and Peræa to Jerusalem, we find ourselves in

[1] Mark iv. 40, οὔπω ἔχετε πίστιν.
[2] Mark ix. 29, cf. Matt. xvii. 20.
[3] Mark xi. 23 ff., πιστεύετε ὅτι ἐλάβετε, καὶ ἔσται ὑμῖν.

quite another atmosphere, and the teaching accordingly is of another character. The audience was differently constituted from that which gathered round our Lord in Galilee. In the Temple-courts, as on the shores of the Lake, a crowd speedily assembled wherever the Master was to be seen and heard, but it contained elements which were not present in Galilee—townsfolk from the Tyropœon, and pilgrims from the Dispersion in many lands, as well as peasants from the rural parts of Palestine. And on the fringe of the crowd, now and again coming to the front with simulated homage [1] or captious questions, were members of the Sanhedrin, not Scribes only or elected counsellors, but the heads of the Priesthood, who, Sadducees as they were, now joined hands with the Pharisees in a determined effort to entrap the great Teacher. Our Lord's answers are preserved, together with a few fragments of His teaching addressed to the multitude, and they form a series of judgements which exhibit His attitude toward a variety of subjects debated in His

[1] Luke xx. 20, ὑποκρινομένους ἑαυτοὺς δικαίους εἶναι.

own generation. We learn in this way His view of certain uses to which the Temple-courts were put; of the claim of the Roman government upon the allegiance of Jews who were under it; of the rejection by the Sadducees of the Pharisaic doctrine of the Resurrection; of the relative importance of the duties prescribed by the Law.[1] His answers not only silenced His adversaries at the time, but asserted certain broad principles which still illuminate life and thought. But even more important are the few final words which He said about Himself. He implies that the authority which He exercised was from above;[2] He refers to Himself as the only and beloved Son of the Owner of the Vineyard,[3] and as the Stone which was declared to be the "Head of the Corner";[4] He calls attention to the paradox that the Christ, though the Son of David, is also his Lord;[5] and at length, when interrogated by the High Priest, He explicitly confesses Him-

[1] Mark xi. 17, xii. 15-17, 24-27, 29-31.
[2] Mark xi. 29 ff.   [3] Mark xii. 6.
[4] Mark xii. 10.   [5] Mark xii. 35-37.

self to be "the Son of the Blessed," and the ultimate fulfiller of Daniel's vision of the Son of Man who comes with the clouds of heaven.[1]

8. The great eschatological discourse which ends the "day of questions" (Mark xiii.) is unique in more than one respect. It is the only prolonged utterance in the Marcan tradition, and almost the only utterance which deals with the Last Things. Elsewhere the teaching of Christ is singularly free from apocalyptic; it has to do with present duties, with things upon earth and things close at hand.[2] No such reticence is practised here. The Apostles had, according to St. Mark, limited their inquiry to the fall of the City and the Temple,[3] but Christ of His own

[1] Mark xiv. 62. Mark's ἐγώ εἰμι is perhaps not so near to the original as the more characteristic Σὺ εἶπας of Matthew, or Σὺ λέγεις of Luke, but it is doubtless a true interpretation of the Lord's answer.

[2] There is a momentary unveiling of the future in Mark viii. 38, but when James and John ask for places of honour in the Messiah's Kingdom, their thoughts are recalled to the Messiah's sufferings (Mark x. 37 f.).

[3] The words καὶ συντελείας τοῦ αἰῶνος added by St. Matthew have probably arisen from that Evangelist's interpretation of St. Mark's συντελεῖσθαι, seen in the light of the discourse itself.

motion went further afield. It has indeed been maintained by recent scholars that certain portions of this discourse (viz., Mark xiii. 7 f., 14-20, 24-27, 30 f.) are fragments of a primitive apocalypse which have been worked into the original tradition. In favour of this view it is urged that they "stand in no inward relation to the rest of the discourse";[1] but, granting this statement, it proves no more than that the discourse has not been preserved in its original order, or was not all delivered at the same time. Even if these passages are removed, there remains in this remarkable chapter a revelation of certain features in the history of the future Church, ending with the final *parousia;* and this alone places chapter xiii. on a different level from the sayings of chapters i.-xii. But was there not a cause for a new departure of this kind? The end of the Ministry and of the Master's earthly life was at hand; within two months the new society of Christ's disciples would have started on its mission, and "the last hour"[2] have begun. Now, if ever, there was a

[1] Wendt, *Teaching of Jesus*, E. Tr., ii. p. 366 n.
[2] 1 John ii. 18, ἐσχάτη ὥρα ἐστίν.

fitting opportunity for foreshadowing the course of future events, and inspiring hope. Yet apart from the use of certain metaphors borrowed from the Old Testament—the "abomination of desolation," the darkening of sun and moon, the falling of stars from heaven, the coming of the Son of Man in the clouds [1]—the whole story of the great future is told with a reserve which is in marked contrast with the extravagance of other apocalyptic descriptions. The Master is not led by the curiosity of His disciples to fix a time either for the destruction of the City or for the end of the age; His words give no support to the belief that He would return in the lifetime of the first generation; they mention no symbolical numbers which might give ground for idle guesses; they refer to no mystical periods such as those which appear in the Apocalypse of St. John; indeed Jesus disclaims all knowledge of "that day or hour."[2] Such disclosures as He makes are

[1] All these occur in the passages which have been regarded as foreign to our Lord's discourse.
[2] Mark xiii. 32.

made with a practical purpose. "Take heed that no man lead you astray . . . when ye hear of wars and tumults, be not troubled . . . take heed to yourselves . . . watch and pray . . . what I say unto you I say unto all, Watch."[1] These are the notes which are heard throughout the discourse, and they reveal the Master's aim. On this one occasion, just before the end of His course, He desired to illuminate the future for the guidance of His disciples in the coming years. So far as we can judge, His teaching would have been wanting in an important particular if it had contained no such limited apocalypse. Moreover, that the eschatology should come just where it does in His teaching is surely in accordance with the general plan of our Lord's ministry. Each group of utterances is seen to arise naturally out of the circumstances in which it occurs. What could be more natural than that the one eschatological discourse should be reserved to the end?

10. The last charge of the risen Lord to

[1] Mark xiii. 5, 7, 9, 23, 33, 35, 37.

the eleven and the future Church is preserved by St. Matthew only,[1] but it may have stood in the original ending of St. Mark, and it forms an apt conclusion to the teaching of the Second Gospel. Once again, as in the first days of the Galilean ministry, Jesus strikes the note of "authority"; but the authority which He now claims is universal, embracing things in heaven as well as things on earth.[2] As He Himself had in those days made disciples and taught them, so He now commits to the Apostles and the Church the task of "discipling" and teaching the nations. But the disciples they made were to be His and not theirs, and their teaching was to be but an enforcing of precepts which they had received from His lips. The mission of the Church must seek its inspiration in the words of the Master, and its strength in His invisible presence, which He pledged Himself to continue until the end of the age.

[1] Matt. xxviii. 18–20. For a further treatment of this passage by the present writer see *Expositor*, Series vi., vol. vi., p. 241.

[2] ἐν οὐρανῷ καὶ ἐπὶ τῆς γῆς. Contrast Mark ii. 10.

It is improbable that the sayings in the Marcan tradition were selected or arranged with the definite intention of representing the teaching of Christ as an ordered whole. Yet we have found in them an order, a purpose, and a relative completeness which suggest that they are in fact fairly representative of the great lines of our Lord's teaching in Galilee and during the last week at Jerusalem. And they exhibit certain characteristics which stand out in clear relief, and which it may be worth while here briefly to note.

(a) We are struck by the *inwardness* of the teaching. The heart, the centre of the moral life in man, is the field in which Jesus sets Himself to work. Repentance and faith, renunciation of self-love, obedience, sacrifice, are the conditions of life under the Kingdom of God. The seed of the Kingdom lives and grows and yields fruit only when it is lodged in good ground. External things, whether ceremonial acts or national power or wealth and place, may be stumbling-blocks in the soul's way to God. All sins come from within, and it is within that the work of purification must begin. The value of a gift is independent of its money-worth, and proportionate to the spiritual effort which it represents.

(*b*) But with this inwardness there is joined in the teaching of Christ an intensely *practical direction*. It is wholly free from the error of regarding external things as indifferent because they are valueless apart from the Spirit. Jesus was precise in His directions with regard to marriage and divorce; He cleansed the Temple from a traffic which was the symbol and occasion of a selfish greed, and refused to allow the house of prayer to be made a thoroughfare; He instituted sacramental actions for perpetual observance in His Church. While His teaching rested on the broad principles of moral and spiritual truth, it could descend to small matters when a principle was even remotely involved. One of His sayings made all meats clean;[1] another has blessed infancy and childhood for all time. His charge to the Twelve enters into trifles connected with food and clothing; when the child of Jairus awoke from her death-sleep, He "commanded that

[1] Mark vii. 19 (reading καθαρίζων with ℵABLΔ).

something should be given her to eat." Nothing was overlooked because it was in itself trivial or external, if it could be made to serve the good of man or the Kingdom of God.

(c) Although delivered under conditions which limited its immediate scope, the teaching possesses an *universality* which strikes even the casual reader. The Master is the Son of Man, and His words are for all men. Quite early in the ministry such sayings as "The Son of Man hath power on earth to forgive sins," "The Sabbath was made for man," "Out of the heart of man evil thoughts proceed," look far beyond the narrow limits of Galilee and of Judaism. The parable of the Sower was addressed to simple people amongst agricultural surroundings, and, as many a country clergyman knows, it appeals with special force to the farmer and the ploughman of rural England to-day; yet the picture which it draws of the various fortunes experienced by the word of God in human hearts is a heritage for all mankind. There is scarcely a saying in the Marcan teaching which is not of far-reaching significance, charged with a lesson for one or more of those types of human character which are always with us.

(*d*) Simple and unpretending as the sayings are, they possess a tone of *authority* which is without parallel in literature. If the Lord does not often in the Second Gospel preface His teaching by the solemn ἀμὴν λέγω ὑμῖν,[1] throughout the book His words carry conviction or at least command attention. Not a hesitating note is struck from the day when He begins, "The Kingdom of God is at hand" to the last scene when He proclaims, "All power hath been given unto Me in heaven and on earth"; He speaks at all times with the same absolute conviction and consciousness of His Divine right. There is majesty in His least utterance, and it is nowhere more easily recognised than in the unvarnished record of the Gospel according to St. Mark.

[1] It occurs only twice in the Galilean teaching (Mark iii. 28, viii. 12), and eleven times in the rest of the Gospel.

THE NON-MARCAN TEACHING IN
ST. MATTHEW

CHAPTER III

THE NON-MARCAN TEACHING IN ST. MATTHEW

BESIDE the memoirs which were the chief source of St. Mark's Gospel the Apostolic age possessed at least another body of tradition, in which the Lord's teaching was more fully represented. Whether this second cycle is to be identified with the "oracles" attributed by Papias to the Apostle Matthew,[1] we need not stop to inquire; certainly it was largely used by the writer of our First Gospel. To the Matthæan tradition, as we will venture to call it, our attention must now be turned.

[1] Eus. *H. E.* iii. 39: Ματθαῖος μὲν οὖν Ἑβραΐδι διαλέκτῳ τὰ λόγια συνεγράψατο. On λόγια see Dean Armitage Robinson's *Study of the Gospels*, p. 69 f.; Stanton, *Gospels*, i., p. 53 f.

68   TEACHING OF OUR LORD

1. The most extensive collection of sayings in the Synoptic Gospels is that which in Augustine's time [1] had already received the title of the "Sermon on the Mount." The name is misleading if it suggests a formal discourse, or even a κήρυγμα addressed to the crowd who hung about our Lord's person. The "Sermon" was, in fact, an instruction or a series of instructions intended, as both St. Matthew and St. Luke are careful to say,[2] for the disciples who formed the inner circle of His audience.[3] It is a specimen, not of Christ's public preaching, but of His manner of teaching those who acknowledged Him as their Master. Moreover, it does not belong to the first days of the Galilean ministry, as its early place in the Gospel of St. Matthew might

---

[1] See the opening words of his *De sermone Domini in monte*.

[2] Matt. v. 1 : ἰδὼν δὲ τοὺς ὄχλους ἀνέβη εἰς τὸ ὄρος, καὶ καθίσαντος αὐτοῦ, προσῆλθον αὐτῷ οἱ μαθηταὶ αὐτοῦ καὶ . . . ἐδίδασκεν αὐτούς. Luke vi. 20 : ἐπάρας τοὺς ὀφθαλμοὺς εἰς τοὺς μαθητὰς αὐτοῦ ἔλεγεν κ.τ.λ.

[3] That it was delivered in the hearing of the multitude, appears from Matt. vii. 28, Luke vii. 1 ; but they were not primarily in view.

lead us to suppose, but rather, as St. Luke's more chronological arrangement makes evident, to the days which followed the choice of the Twelve.[1] By that time the Lord's popularity had perhaps reached its highest point, and the crowd which followed Him was daily replenished by fresh arrivals from all parts of Syria and the adjacent lands;[2] while on the other hand His breach with the official teachers of Israel was practically complete.[3] The moment was opportune for gathering the whole body of His adherents together, and promulgating the fundamental laws of the new Kingdom. Ancient writers compare or contrast the Sermon with the Lawgiving. On both occasions the scene was a mountain, and the voice Divine. But the Lawgiving was attended by circumstances of terror, while the Sermon opens with beatitudes; the Decalogue

---

[1] Cf. Luke vi. 12 ff., vii. 1 ; in Mark there is a manifest break (at iii. 19b), where it is easy to fit the teaching in the hill-country.

[2] Mark iii. 7, Luke vi. 17, ὄχλος πολὺς μαθητῶν αὐτοῦ και πλῆθος πολὺ τοῦ λαοῦ.

[3] Mark iii. 6.

was written on tables of stone, whereas Christ was content to inscribe His new law on the memory and the heart. The parallel, however, is closer and deeper than at first sight it may appear to be. In the Sermon our Lord is not merely the Teacher, but the Legislator; it is in great part a code of laws enacted by Him on the strength of His personal authority. The power (ἐξουσία) which at an earlier stage had revealed itself in authoritative teaching and miraculous working is now manifested in legislative acts. Six times in one chapter Christ overrules an old enactment by a new one which rests on His own word.[1] Yet the New Law is not a rival of the Law of Mount Sinai, but its complement.[2] Jesus had not come to break down the ancient barriers which protected human life from the inroad of the selfish passions, but to introduce principles of conduct which would gradually supersede the necessity of legal restraints. If His disciples were to be no longer "under law,"

[1] The remarkable formula ἠκούσατε ὅτι ἐρρέθη τοῖς ἀρχαίοις . . ἐγὼ δὲ λέγω ὑμῖν occurs with slight variations in Matt. v. 21 f., 27 f., 31 f., 33 f., 38 f., 43 f.

[2] Matt. v. 17: οὐκ ἦλθον καταλῦσαί ἀλλὰ πληρῶσαι.

it was because they would be "led by the Spirit" which instinctively fulfils the Law.[1] "That which was said to the ancients" is definitely set aside by Christ only when, through the hardness or dulness of the times, the earlier legislation had been unable to give effect to the fulness of the Divine Will.[2]

From the precepts of the ancient Law the Lord proceeds to deal with the "righteousness,"[3] *i.e.*, the religious practice, of His own age, which is treated under the three heads of almsgiving, prayer, and fasting.[4] Here, again, He is careful not to disturb existing landmarks unnecessarily; it was enough to correct what was amiss and supply what was wanting at the time. The "righteousness of the Scribes and Pharisees" was insufficient, and it was defaced

---

[1] Gal. v. 18 ; Rom. viii. 4.

[2] Thus, *e.g.*, the regulation of Deut. xxiv. 1, which Christ withdraws in Matt. v. 32, was in His judgement a temporary concession to the σκληροκαρδία of Israel, made with the purpose of limiting an evil which at the time could not be suppressed; see the writer's note on Mark x. 5.

[3] Matt. vi. 1 (reading δικαιοσύνην with ℵ^b BD).

[4] Matt. vi. 2 ff., 5 ff., 16 ff.

by hypocrisy; but Christ does not propose any radical change in its main features. Almsgiving, prayer, and fasting have their place in the religious life, and He recognises the fact. But in these acts of religion He requires more than the external performance; each is to have its inward and spiritual side, turned towards the Father of spirits and looking to His approval for its only recompense.[1] It is thus that Christian righteousness is to "exceed"[2] the righteousness of the Synagogue —not in the multiplicity of its acts, but in the inwardness and concentration of its spirit. How little importance is ascribed by Christ to mere quantity in religious actions is apparent from the model[3] prayer which He gives, in which all the necessities of life are compressed into the fewest words.[4] Even in prayer, the most spiritual of the three chief acts of righteousness, there was danger from ex-

[1] See the refrain in Matt. vi. 4, 6, 18.
[2] Matt. v. 20.
[3] Matt. vi. 9, οὕτως προσεύχεσθε ὑμεῖς.
[4] The Lucan text of the Prayer is even shorter than the form in Matthew, and possibly more primitive.

ternalism; words must needs be used, at least in common prayer, as the vehicle for desires which in themselves are voiceless;[1] but the multiplication of words for the words' sake was no better than a heathenish βατταλογία in the sight of the Father, who needs no such incentive to bestow His gifts.[2]

In the next place Christ insists on that which lies behind all true acts of devotion, the upward trend of mind which finds its goal in the Presence of God. The subject of the Kingdom of Heaven must not seek his treasure on earth. "Mammon"—the word reminds us that the audience is an Aramaic-speaking crowd [3]—may not share his allegiance with God; his one aim must be to gain the Divine Kingdom and righteousness, and earthly things, even the most necessary, should take the second place.[4] Christ's disciple must be free from an anxiety which distracts while it does not satisfy.[5] His

[1] Rom. viii. 26, τὸ πνεῦμα ὑπερεντυγχάνει στεναγμοῖς ἀλαλήτοις.

[2] Matt. vi. 7; cf. vii. 11.

[3] Cf. Aug. *De serm. Domini*, ii. 14, 47, lucrum Punice *mammon* dicitur.

[4] Matt. vi. 33. [5] Matt. vi. 27 ff.

whole life is to be lived upon a higher plane, from which he will be able to see all things in their true proportions.

The Sermon ends with a code of directions for the guidance of daily conduct, which refutes the suspicion of transcendentalism. The Lord charges His disciples to abstain from hasty judgements:[1] to exercise a wise reserve in religious communications with non-Christians:[2] to deal with their brother-men as they would themselves be dealt with by God.[3] They are not to suffer themselves to be carried away by the current of popular opinion or prevalent practice:[4] they are especially to guard against religious teachers whose deeds belie their words.[5] Above all, they are to beware lest their enthusiasm for the Christian cause expend itself in a mere confession of the Name, or even in the bustling activity of outward service. The Lord ends with the warning that His words will profit only those who obey them: the rest of His disciples are as men who build

---

[1] Matt. vii. 1 ff. [2] Matt. vii. 6.
[3] Matt. vii. 12. [4] Matt. vii. 13 ff.
[5] Matt. vii. 15 ff.

their house on the sandy floor of a *wady*, where the first storms of winter will bury them under its ruins.[1]

2. With a characteristic perception of the inner affinity of incidents remote from one another in time and place, St. Matthew brings together in chapter xi.[2] a series of sayings which reveal Christ's view of His own office and person. Teaching of this kind is rare in the Synoptic Gospels, and is therefore peculiarly welcome when it is offered.

The Evangelist begins with the question which reached our Lord from the prison of John the Baptist, now in the dungeons of Machærus. It was brought to Christ, if St. Luke's order is right, shortly after the great miracle at Nain, and not long after the Sermon on the Mount. Such teaching, confirmed by such a miracle, must have deeply stirred the heart of Galilee, and raised in many minds the

[1] Matt. vii. 24 ff.

[2] The corresponding sections in St. Luke are Luke vii. 18-28, xvi. 16, vii. 31-35, x. 13-15, 21 f. The last three verses in St. Matthew (xi. 28-30) have no parallel in St. Luke.

question which the Baptist put into words, Σὺ εἶ ὁ ἐρχόμενος; Christ points the way to the true answer without anticipating it: He places the facts before John and leaves the Baptist to draw the natural inference.[1] This incident probably took place in private, or in the presence of the Twelve only; but the crowd outside was aware of the coming of the Baptist's disciples, and Jesus seized the opportunity of directing attention to the mission of John.[2] John, He taught, was at once greater than any of the Old Testament heroes, and yet inferior in privilege to the least disciple of the Kingdom, since he came to prepare the way of the Kingdom, and therefore himself stood outside its borders.[3] This teaching left no reasonable doubt as to the Lord's own position; if St. John was the last herald of the Advent, who could Jesus be but the Christ? More plainly than this He declined to speak, for He

[1] Matt. xi. 4 ff.

[2] Matt. xi. 7, τούτων δὲ πορευομένων (Luke, ἀπελθόντων δὲ τῶν ἀγγέλων Ἰωάνου) ἤρξατο ὁ Ἰησοῦς λέγειν τοῖς ὄχλοις περὶ Ἰωάνου.

[3] Matt. xi. 11 ff.

recognised in the crowd about Him none of the moral earnestness which would have rendered them capable of grasping a great spiritual truth;[1] they were as children who played with the solemnities of life, and wondered that the Forerunner and the Christ did not share their levity.[2]

So far the First and Third Gospels follow the same order; but at this point St. Matthew, in accordance with his principle of arrangement, goes to another part of his document for the logical sequel. It belongs, as St. Luke shews us, to the narrative of the mission and return of the Seventy, which followed the Lord's final departure from Capernaum.[3] Capernaum and the adjacent lake-side towns had but too fully justified Christ's verdict upon the Galileans of His generation, and the purpose of the new mission seems to have been to awaken in the villages of Peræa and central Palestine a sense of the greatness of the opportunity which Galilee had slighted, and which was now at

---

[1] Matt. xi. 12: βιασταὶ ἁρπάζουσιν αὐτήν.
[2] Matt. xi. 16 ff.
[3] Luke ix. 51, x. 1, 13 ff., 21 ff.

their own doors. The Seventy appear to have met with some success; at all events, they returned flushed with hope, and their enthusiasm stirred in the human heart of Christ a sense of joy which is quite unexampled in the records of His life. He knew that the names of these simple but loyal followers were "written in heaven"; He saw in them the type of some of the best members of His future Church, men of childlike faith, unlettered and without personal weight, yet strong in the possession of a Divine secret which was hidden from the great world.[1] As He realized this vision of the victory of faith, the Lord "exulted in the Holy Spirit"; the "oil of joy" descended upon Him.[2] His "exultation" revealed itself in a solemn act of thanksgiving,[3] and this, uttered doubtless in the presence of the Twelve, passed into the words of self-manifestation to

---

[1] Luke x. 21; cf. 1 Cor. i. 26 ff.

[2] Luke l.c.: ἐν αὐτῇ τῇ ὥρᾳ ἠγαλλιάσατο τῷ πνεύματι τῷ ἁγίῳ. Cf. Heb. i. 9 (Ps. xlv. 7): ἔχρισέν σε ὁ θεός, ὁ θεός σου, ἐλαίῳ ἀγαλλιάσεως παρὰ τοὺς μετόχους σου.

[3] Matt. xi. 25: ἐξομολογοῦμαί σοι, πάτερ κ.τ.λ. ἐξομολογεῖσθαι here of course = הוֹדָה, as in Ps. vii. 17, ix. 1, &c.

IN ST. MATTHEW

which reference has been made. "All things are delivered to Me by My Father, and none knoweth the Son [1] except the Father, nor doth any know the Father [1] except the Son, and he to whomsoever the Son shall choose to reveal Him." [2] As Dr. Sanday remarked thirty years ago, "There is nothing in the Johannean Christology that [this passage] does not cover. Even the doctrine of pre-existence seems to be implicitly contained in it. For how and when is this unique and mutual knowledge to be regarded as obtained? Clearly it is no empirical guessing; it does not appear possible that it should be grounded on anything short of an essential unity." [3] The knowledge claimed is that of a son, and it rests upon sonship; it is a strange misreading of the words which reverses this order, as Professor Harnack seems to do, when he bases Christ's consciousness of sonship

[1] St. Luke writes: "who is the Son" "who is the Father," a paraphrase which is true but not exhaustive of the sense, and not structurally necessary (cf. Matt. vii. 16, 20, &c., where ἐπιγινώσκειν τινά occurs).

[2] Matt. xi. 27.

[3] Sanday, *Authorship and Historical Character of the Fourth Gospel* (London, 1872), p. 109.

80   TEACHING OF OUR LORD

upon His knowledge of the Father.[1] It is not knowledge which makes Him "the Son," but His Sonship which enables Him to know. He declares that He knows God as only a son can know his father, and that this knowledge is not a possession which other sons of God [2] naturally share with Him, but one which belongs of right to Him alone, and is vouchsafed to others only so far as He is pleased to impart it. This is to claim not only unique knowledge, but unique sonship. It is difficult to discover any essential difference between this statement in St. Matthew and the closing words of St. John's prologue: "God none hath seen at any time; God only begotten, who is in the bosom of the Father, He declared Him." [3]

The exquisite invitation to the "weary and

[1] Harnack, *Das Wesen des Christentums*, p. 81 (= Saunders, E. Tr., p. 127 f.).

[2] Cf. Matt. xvii. 26.

[3] Let the reader compare the two passages and judge for himself:—

Matt. xi. 17.
οὐδὲ τὸν πατέρα τις ἐπιγινώσκει εἰ μὴ ὁ υἱὸς καὶ ᾧ ἐὰν βούληται ὁ υἱὸς ἀποκαλύψαι.

John i. 18.
Θεὸν οὐδεὶς ἑώρακεν πώποτε. μονογενὴς Θεός, ὁ ὢν εἰς τὸν κόλπον τοῦ πατρός, ἐκεῖνος ἐξηγήσατο.

heavy laden," which in St. Matthew follows the ἀγαλλίασις,[1] may well have been spoken on another occasion. It seems to require the presence of a crowd of toil-worn peasants, bringing their sick to be healed, or pressing round the Christ with wistful faces and half-formed longings for His help. Yet no reader of the Gospels will wish to dislodge this saying from the place which the consummate skill of the Evangelist has found for it. If the words of ver. 27 lift the Son to a height where none may approach Him, in His δεῦτε πρὸς μέ He steps down once more to our level, and He to whom all things are delivered, and who alone knows God, shews Himself the sympathetic friend of suffering humanity. Yet the note of authority, of ownership, of superhuman greatness, can still be heard: "Take my yoke, learn from Me; I will give you rest." It is the voice of the Only-begotten Son; we recall Augustine's words: "Fecisti nos ad Te, et inquietum est cor nostrum donec requiescat in Te."[2]

[1] Matt. xi. 28–30. St. Luke has no parallel.
[2] *Confessions*, i. 1.

3. Twice in the First Gospel [1] the Lord speaks of the future Christian Society, using the word ἐκκλησία. The two passages, which we will bring together here, contain important teaching on the powers and responsibilities of the Church.

The first is the famous promise to St. Peter, "Thou art Peter (Πέτρος), and upon this rock (πέτρα) I will build My Church." Christ has already used, in the Sermon on the Mount,[2] the metaphor of building upon a rock. There it denotes the security which the individual life attains by obedience to the words of Christ; here the building is not an individual but a congregation, Christ Himself is the builder, and the rock appears to be St. Peter, representing the whole Apostolate.[3] For the

---

[1] Matt. xvi. 18 f.; xviii. 15–20.

[2] Matt. vii. 24: ᾠκοδόμησεν αὐτοῦ τὴν οἰκίαν ἐπὶ τὴν πέτραν.

[3] He had spoken on behalf of all in answer to the question, Ὑμεῖς δὲ τίνα με λέγετε εἶναι (Matt. xvi. 15; Mark viii. 29). Peter's name supplied an apt image of the relation which the Twelve were called to fulfil towards all future generations of disciples; cf. Eph. ii. 20: ἐποικοδομηθέντες ἐπὶ τῷ θεμελίῳ τῶν ἀποστόλων καὶ προφητῶν. Apoc. xxi. 14: τὸ τεῖχος τῆς πόλεως ἔχον θεμελίους δώδεκα, καὶ ἐπ' αὐτῶν δώδεκα ὀνόματα τῶν δώδεκα ἀποστόλων τοῦ ἀρνίου.

IN ST. MATTHEW

aggregate of successive generations of the faithful St. Matthew employs the word which in the Greek Old Testament represents עֵדָה or קָהָל,[1] the "congregation" of Israel; and Christ probably used the Aramaic equivalent. In so doing He created a new Israel, substituting the congregation of His disciples for "Israel after the flesh," which knew Him not.[2] Israel was "the congregation of Jehovah," and the Christian brotherhood bears in the Epistles of St. Paul the corresponding title, "the Church (or the churches) of God."[3] But Christ does not hesitate to speak of the new congregation as His own (οἰκοδομήσω μου τὴν ἐκκλησίαν). No such claim is attributed to Moses, whose relation to Israel was that of a servant set over the House of God. Jesus speaks as the Master and owner of the house; the Church of God is His, since He is the Son and the Heir of God.[4]

[1] Cf. Hort, *Ecclesia*, p. 3 ff.

[2] Cf. Rom. ii. 28, ix. 6 f.; Gal. vi. 16; Apoc. iii. 9.

[3] 1 Cor. i. 2, xv. 9; 2 Cor. i. 2; Gal. i. 13; 1 Thess. ii. 14. Αἱ ἐκκλησίαι τοῦ χριστοῦ occurs, however, in Rom. xvi. 16.

[4] Heb. iii. 6; see Westcott's note.

Not less remarkable are the words that follow: "the gates of Hades shall not prevail against it."[1] Human institutions, one after another, fall under the power of dissolution, and pass into oblivion, or become memories of the past. Christ foresaw that the society which He was founding was destined to outlive every other organization upon earth; the day would never come which should see its downfall or disappearance. History has thus far fulfilled this prophecy, and Christians are entitled to believe that it will hold true to the end. An institution which has survived the Roman Empire and the governments that rose upon its ruins, can await without fear any changes that time may work in the existing order of the world.

We will pass to the second occasion on which the Lord referred to the Ecclesia.[2] It is pre-

---

[1] For πύλαι Ἅδου cf. Isa. xxxviii. 10 (LXX) and 3 Macc. v. 52. The Risen Christ has the keys of Hades (Apoc. i. 18) and can liberate the dead. But the imagery in Matt. *l.c.* goes further: Hades prevails against the individual, though in the end it will be forced to set him free; but the Church as a body can defy its power altogether.

[2] Matt. xviii. 15 ff.

carious to build chronological inferences on St. Matthew's order, but it may probably be assumed in this instance that the second reference is later than the first; certainly it fits in well with the context where it occurs. The Lord had spoken much of the danger of placing a stumblingblock in the way of a brother. But what if a brother be the offender? are you to connive at his trespass? No, he must be brought to see and confess the fault. Private remonstrance is to be tried first, and if this fails, remonstrance in the presence of two or three witnesses; as a last resource, the matter must be referred to the congregation, whose judgement is to be final. Should the offending brother refuse to listen to the congregation, he puts himself outside the pale of Christian fellowship, and may be regarded as the Jew regarded the pagan or the outcast.[1] The

[1] ἔστω σοι ὥσπερ ὁ ἐθνικὸς καὶ ὁ τελώνης, *i.e.*, as the ἀποσυνάγωγος (John ix. 22; xii. 42; xvi. 2) was regarded by the Jewish community. But the ἐκκλησία can scarcely itself be the Jewish community, though Dr. Hort (*Ecclesia*, p. 10) inclines to this view; there is no example of this use of the word in the N.T., and its meaning here is surely governed by c. xvi. 18.

principle affirmed is merely the inherent right of a society to exclude a member who declines to submit to its ruling. This power was exercised by the Synagogue, and Christ claims no less for His Church. But the next words reach much further: "Whatsoever things ye bind on earth shall be bound in heaven, and whatsoever ye loose on earth shall be loosed in heaven." "Binding" and "loosing" are terms borrowed from the Synagogue; the Rabbis were said to bind what they forbade, and to loose what they allowed;[1] and Jesus transfers this judicial power to the Christian Ecclesia, which was in future to be the judge in questions of religious belief and practice. But he does much more, for he declares that the decisions of the Church shall be ratified in heaven. The promise which had been made to the Apostolate in the person of St. Peter is now extended to the whole body of the Church.[2] Not

[1] Abundant instances of this use of אסר and התיר will be found in J. Lightfoot's *Horae Hebraicae* (ed. Goudell), ii. p. 237 ff.

[2] Matt. xvi. 19: ὃ ἐὰν δήσῃς . . . ὃ ἐὰν λύσῃς; Matt. xviii. 18; ὅσα ἐὰν δήσητε . . . ὅσα ἐὰν λύσητε.

the Apostolate only but the whole Church was to be the organ of the Holy Spirit, and the Spirit speaking through the Church would pronounce judgments which should be binding alike on earth and in heaven. The human infirmity which is so conspicuous in the history of the Church sufficiently explains her frequent failures in the attempt to reach this high ideal. Great Church councils have arrived at decisions which it is impossible to regard as ratified by the judgement of God. Yet it is not too much to say that what the universal conscience of Christendom has affirmed does bear the stamp of Divine approval, whilst that which all faithful Christians reprobate is assuredly "bound" in heaven. *Quod ubique, quod semper, quod ab omnibus* [1] is a maxim which enshrines a great truth; the voice of the whole Christian people in all time is the Voice of God.

But the Church has another privilege which can be exercised by the smallest of Christian congregations. "Where two or three are gathered together in My Name, there am I

[1] Vincentius Lirinensis, *Commonitorum*, 2.

in the midst of them."[1] The promise is still to the Church, not to the individual;[2] that its fulfilment may be claimed, there must be at least two disciples acting in Christian fellowship, and thus representing the whole body. But this *minimum* is assured of Christ's presence as well as the largest congregation; for the purposes of common prayer it possesses the privileges of the body, provided that it be gathered in Christ's Name.[3] Christ's "there am I" necessarily involves the coming of the Spirit, thus again antici-

[1] Matt. xviii. 20.

[2] The Matthæan saying is thus distinct from the Oxyrhynchan *logion;* see Grenfell and Hunt, *Oxyrhynchus Papyri*, vol. i. p. 3: [λέγ]ει ['Ιησοῦς, "Οπ]ου ἐὰν ὦσιν [β, οὐκ] ε[ἰσὶ]ν ἄθεοι, καὶ [ὅ]που [ε]ἷς ἐστιν μόνος, [λέ]γω, ἐγώ εἰμι μετ' αὐτοῦ.

[3] Cf. Tertullian, *De cast.* 7, "Sed ubi tres ecclesia est, licet laici." He might have written "ubi duo," for he read the passage as we do (*præscr.* 16, *ad uxor.* ii. 9). And he overlooks εἰς τὸ ἐμὸν ὄνομα, which guards against the sectarian spirit that prefers the company of two or three. The *à fortiori* claim upon this promise of the regular assemblies of the Church is well urged in the original of the "Prayer of St. Chrysostom"; see Brightman, *Liturgies*, i. p. 367, ὁ τὰς κοινὰς ταύτας καὶ συμφώνους ἡμῖν χαρισάμενος προσευχάς, ὁ καὶ δυσὶ καὶ τρισὶ κ.τ.λ.

pating the fuller treatment of the Fourth Gospel. Only when the Spirit had been sent from the Father in the Son's Name did it become possible for the Lord to be in the midst of every congregation of His Church to the end of time.[1] The Ascension and the Pentecost have illuminated a saying which to those who first heard it must have been perplexing indeed.

4. Our Lord's teaching, as represented in the Matthæan tradition, places in contrast with the Ecclesia the world in its two aspects, as the visible order of the universe (κόσμος), and as the course of human affairs under the conditions of time (αἰών).[2]

Christ manifests no hostility to the world in either sense. The visible world is the harvest-field in which He sees the ripening crops awaiting His labourers; from another point of view, the harvest is the end of the world, and the

---

[1] Cf. Matt. xxviii. 20.

[2] Dalman, who observes that Matthew alone of the Synoptists uses κόσμος freely, shows that in the Jewish literature עולם cover both senses (*Worte Jesu*, i. pp. 136, 138, 140 = E. Tr. pp. 167, 169, 171).

reapers are not Apostles and Evangelists, but the angels who will attend His coming.[1] If His own countrymen and His own generation afforded little ground for hope, or indeed seemed likely to go from bad to worse,[2] His eye saw the Gentile nations flocking into the Kingdom from the four quarters of the earth.[3] The present age must reach its appointed end;[4] but Jesus expects a new world to take the place of the old, and a regeneration of heaven and earth analogous to the new birth which ushers individual lives into the Kingdom of God.[5] His outlook is therefore, upon the whole, full of hope; the present state of mixed good and evil will issue, He foresees, in the final triumph of good.

[1] Matt. ix. 37 f., xiii. 37, 39.

[2] Matt. xii. 39-45.

[3] Matt. viii. 11; cf. Luke xiii. 29.

[4] The συντέλεια τοῦ αἰῶνος is mentioned five times by St. Matthew (xiii. 39, 40, 49; xxiv. 3; xxviii. 20), and in this sense by St. Matthew only.

[5] Matt. xix. 28. For παλινγενεσία see Tit. iii. 5, and cf. John iii. 5; in Matt. the term seems to be equivalent to the ἀποκατάστασις πάντων mentioned in Acts iii. 21 though Dalman (p. 145 f.) denies this.

IN ST. MATTHEW

Yet Jesus does not minimize either the extent to which evil prevails in the world as it now is, or the seriousness of the issues which it entails. The latter point is brought out with great variety of illustration in the Matthæan parables, which, when all allowances have been made for the high colouring of Eastern imagery, leave no doubt as to the general purport of Christ's teaching on the subject. The angel-reapers "shall gather out of His Kingdom those that work lawlessness, and shall cast them into the furnace of fire"; [1] "there," it is twice said, "shall be the weeping and the gnashing of teeth."[1] The angel-fishers in the sea of life "shall cast the worthless outside"; [2] the Master will deliver the debtor who has been forgiven, but has proved himself unworthy, into the hands of the ministers of torture, until he shall have paid the whole; [3] the guest who is not suitably attired for the wedding feast is to be

---

[1] Matt. xiii. 30, 42: Ὁ κλαυθμός, ὁ βρυγμός (so also in viii. 12, xxii. 13, xxiv. 5, xxv. 30; Luke xiii. 28), misery which is such κατ' ἐξοχήν.

[2] Matt. xiii. 48: τὰ δὲ σαπρὰ ἔξω ἔβαλον.

[3] Matt. xviii. 34.

cast out of the banqueting-hall into the darkness of the night;[1] the virgin attendants of the Bride who let their lamps die down will find the door shut against a diligence which has come too late;[2] the slave who has neglected his talent, though but one was committed to him, not only loses it, but is cast out from his Lord's presence.[3] These scenes represent the fate of disloyal or negligent disciples, but the final parable extends the principle, *mutatis mutandis*, to all mankind. In all nations of the world those who have failed to serve Christ by ministering to His brethren, their fellow-men, must go away from the judgement seat into age-long punishment.[4] The general import of this teaching is too plain to be disputed; beyond a doubt the Lord points to loss and suffering of the gravest kind as the lot of those who sin against the light they posesss, or neglect their opportunities of doing good.

---

[1] Matt. xxii. 18: εἰς τὸ σκότος τὸ ἐξώτερον. Cf. John xiii. 30, where it is significantly said of Judas, ἐκεῖνος ἐξῆλθεν εὐθύς· ἦν δὲ νύξ.

[2] Matt. xxv. 11.

[3] Matt. xxv. 29 f.   [4] Matt. xxv. 46.

The Matthæan teaching possesses all the features which we have observed in the Marcan tradition.; the same inwardness, practical bent, universality of application, majesty of manner, are apparent in both records; the same unique personality can be recognised in both. But the field of observation is larger in St. Matthew than in St. Mark; the range of subjects embraced by the teaching is more varied, and the teaching itself more extended and less fragmentary. We are therefore in a better position for gaining a conception of our Lord's scope and purpose as a Teacher, and we see Him in some lights which are quite new. He appears, as we have learnt, in the character of a legislator; and we notice the wisdom with which, while conserving for the time a system which could not be at once abandoned, He aims at substituting for mechanical obedience the great principles of morality and religion which lie at the root of all true goodness. He reveals Himself also in the light of a great architect, a constructive mind which could plan and lay the foundations of a spiritual building destined to last as long as the world itself. We are struck again by the width of His outlook on human life; His appreciation of the forces which are struggling for mastery in the world; His calm anticipation of the end, and the richness and variety of the imagery adopted in order to impress upon an unspiritual age the gravity of the issues to which time is carrying the race and each individual man. Lastly, in an hour of unexampled exultation, He reveals to us that which lay behind all His teaching and all His life, the secret source of Divine knowledge which belonged to Him as the Only-begotten Son. We catch but a momentary glimpse of the mystery of His relation to God, but it is enough to send us back to the Gospels with a deeper sense of the graciousness of One who, possessing a perfect knowledge of God, condescended to teach men the elements of spiritual truth.

THE TEACHING PECULIAR TO
ST. LUKE

CHAPTER IV

THE TEACHING PECULIAR TO ST. LUKE

IT has been calculated that out of a total of 1,149 verses the Gospel of St. Luke has 499 which are peculiar to itself, *i.e.*, consisting of matter not to be found in St. Matthew or St. Mark.[1] Of these peculiarly Lucan verses 261, or rather more than half, contain sayings of our Lord. It is needless, for our present purpose, to inquire what proportion of the Lucan sayings came from the non-Marcan document which was also at the disposal of St. Matthew, or to what other sources St. Luke had access, especially in that great section of his Gospel[2] which is almost wholly independent of the other Synoptists, and to which nearly

---

[1] Sir J. C. Hawkins, *Horae Synopticae*, p. 23.
[2] Luke ix. 51–xviii. 14.

three-fourths of his sayings belong. In any case we are indebted to this Evangelist for a large and most important contribution to our knowledge of the teaching of Christ.

1. The Lucan tradition, like the Marcan, contains no great sermon or prolonged instruction. On one occasion St. Luke seems to be on the point of reporting a synagogue address delivered at Nazareth,[1] but either from lack of information or for other reasons he contents himself with its opening and closing words. The most characteristic feature of the Lucan teaching is its wealth of parable. No fewer than fifteen, or if we add three minor similitudes, eighteen,[2] of the Synoptic parables are due to St. Luke, and they occupy more than a twelfth part of his Gospel. The importance of this contribution becomes still more evident when we remember that it includes such parables as the Good Samaritan, the Great Supper, the Prodigal Son, the Rich Man and Lazarus, the Pharisee and the Publican. Not only are these stories full of a

[1] Luke iv. 21 ff.
[2] Plummer, *St. Luke*, p. xli.

beauty which has fascinated all who have ever listened to them, but they add a new element to the teaching of our Lord, and possess a character which readily distinguishes them from the parables of St. Matthew and St. Mark.

The Marcan and nearly all the Matthæan parables form part of Christ's public teaching, and are designed to illustrate the origin, growth, and consummation of the Kingdom of God. The parables which are peculiar to St. Luke belong to another type. Not one of them opens with the formula ὁμοία ἐστιν ἡ βασιλεία τῶν οὐρανῶν or τοῦ θεοῦ[1]; few if any of them belong to the public ministry. They are taken, as it seems, from recollections of His private conversation with the Twelve or with others who were about Him, and they deal with the subjects of religious interest upon which the conversation happened to turn. Thus the parable of the Good Samaritan is an answer to the casual question, "And who is my neighbour?";[2] the parable of the Rich Fool arises out of a request which revealed the

[1] "The Kingdom of Heaven (or, of God) is like unto . . ."
[2] Luke x. 29, cp. 30, ὑπολαβὼν ὁ Ἰησοῦς εἶπεν.

worldly-mindedness of one of His audience;[1] the parable of the Great Supper, out of the inopportune remark, "Happy is he who shall eat bread in the Kingdom of God."[2] The three parables of chapter xv. appear to be a reply to the muttered complaint of the Pharisees that the Lord received sinners and ate with them;[3] the parable of the Pharisee and Publican was elicited by the uncharitableness of certain pretenders to sanctity who had crossed our Lord's path;[4] the Widow and Judge was intended to sustain the flagging zeal of some who were growing weary of unanswered prayer.[5] The surroundings were not less various. Two of the Lucan parables were spoken at suppers where Jesus was an invited guest;[6] others, probably the greater number, while He walked along the high road with His disciples, or stood for a while in a village street surrounded by a crowd. Under these circumstances the parable was turned to a purpose distinct from that which it had served in the preaching

[1] Luke xii. 13.
[2] Luke xiv. 15.
[3] Luke xv. 2.
[4] Luke xviii. 9.
[5] Luke xviii. 1.
[6] Luke vii. 36 ff., xiv. 15 ff.

of the Kingdom; it became the vehicle of religious conversation, enriching and illuminating the ordinary intercourse of life. This fact not only illustrates the boundless fecundity of the mind which was capable of pouring out such treasures without premeditation, but it also explains the wider scope and the greater human interest which belong to the parables of the Third Gospel.

The teaching of the Lucan parables, as their origin and purpose would have led us to expect, chiefly concerns the individual life. It is not the world or the Church which is in view so much as the individual soul, with its separate needs and responsibilities. The lost sheep is one of a flock, the lost coin one of a purseful; the angels rejoice over one sinner that repents. In almost every parable there is a hero whose individuality arrests the attention—the lone traveller on the Jericho road, the beggar who lies sore and starving on the rich man's doorstep, the widow who cries till she is avenged, the publican who stands far off with downcast eyes; and often the story is applied by our Lord to the personal life—"thou fool, this night thy soul shall be required of thee": "go and do thou likewise": "he that humbleth himself shall be exalted."

What, then, are the salient points in this teaching of Christ upon the subject of personal religion which gives to St. Luke's parables their distinctive character? In the first place it emphasizes the need of spiritual restoration which is the *raison d'être* of our Lord's mission. The sheep, the coin, the son, lost but capable of being found again, represent in three different aspects the human soul estranged from God by sin; while the Divine grace which brings it back is seen in the threefold image of the Shepherd, the Woman, and the Father. This great trilogy of parables is a treasury upon which preachers and guides of souls will draw as long as the world lasts; and with it may be classed the Great Supper, which foretells the catholicity of the Church's mission, and the Two Debtors, which shews the response elicited by the love of God when it is believed. Taken together, these five parables cover the whole history of human salvation and anticipate the soteriology of St. Paul and St. John.

PECULIAR TO ST. LUKE

A second group illuminates the mystery of Prayer. Two of the three parables which deal with Prayer, the Midnight Visitor[1] and the Importunate Widow,[2] set forth a condition of successful prayer to which Christ evidently attached supreme importance, the spirit of absolute conviction and resolute determination[3] to gain the desired end. The Lord Himself brings out the point of this pair of parables: if importunity conquered the selfishness of the sleeping householder and the indifference of the unscrupulous judge, how much more surely will it avail with One whose delays are due only to the long-suffering of an infinite life and a prescient love![4] The third parable on Prayer[5] calls attention to another condition which is no less essential. To the persistence of the importunate suppliant there must be added the publican's sense of personal unworthiness. The claim which Prayer makes upon God is that of utter need, not of justice or right; con-

---

[1] Luke xi. 5–8. [2] Luke xviii. 1–8.
[3] Luke xi. 8 διὰ τὴν ἀναιδίαν αὐτοῦ ἐγερθεὶς δώσει. xviii. 5 διά γε τὸ παρέχειν μοι κόπον ἐκδικήσω αὐτήν.
[4] Luke xi. 13, xviii. 6–8. [5] Luke xviii. 9–14.

sciousness of sin and of the need of mercy must supplement and chasten the boldness and pertinacity which proceed from faith in the Divine love and power.

A third series of parables relates to Service. A fig-tree planted within the fenced enclosure of a vineyard,[1] if it fails to respond to its opportunities and bears no fruit from year to year, must ultimately be cut down; it wastes (καταργεῖ) good ground which might have been occupied by the vine. So the spiritual opportunities of a nation or an individual are forfeited by continued neglect of service, though not until every effort of the great ἀμπελουργός has been in vain. Another parable[2] represents the servants of Christ (δούλους ἑαυτοῦ) as entrusted with a *mina* each, their use of this relatively small sum[3] determining their eventual position in His Kingdom. Here the relation between present service and the future life comes into sight, and light is thrown upon the

[1] Luke xiii. 6–9; cf. Mark xii. 1.
[2] Luke xix. 12–27.
[3] The "talent" of the similar parable in Matt. xxv. 14 ff. was equivalent to sixty *minae*.

famous *agraphon* which Bishop Westcott took for the motto of more than one of his earlier works, Γίνεσθε τραπεζῖται δόκιμοι, "Prove yourselves good bankers." Lastly, lest the inference should be drawn that the reward is not κατὰ χάριν but κατὰ ὀφείλημα,[1] the disciple of St. Paul is careful to add a third illustration which teaches that when all has been done the servants of God are "unprofitable" to Him.[2] God could have dispensed with their service and have been no poorer; if He accepts and requires it, He does so for their sake, because service is the necessary condition of true blessedness.

The four remaining parables peculiar to St. Luke set forth the responsibilities and temptations of social life, more especially those which arise in connexion with wealth. The first of this series reproves the folly of "making haste to be rich" at the cost of the highest interests of human nature. In the little story of the Rich Fool[3] Jesus condemns not the

[1] Rom. iv. 4.
[2] Luke xvii. 10, δοῦλοι ἀχρεῖοί ἐσμεν.
[3] Luke xii. 16–21.

acquisition of wealth in itself, but the neglect of Divine riches [1] to which it often leads. No multiplication of material possessions can convert them into the essence of life; [2] at best they are but accidental accretions, which may or may not be a true enrichment of its powers. The parable of the Dishonest Steward exposes another danger which attends the commercial spirit—the fraudulence that under the name of business creeps into the relations of men of the world. But its chief purpose is to claim for the service of God the best side of the worldly wisdom so often displayed in transactions of this kind, its φρονιμότης, the intelligence and quickness of observation, the good sense and promptness in action which its manifests. Our Lord would isolate this property, in itself a valuable one, from unworthy surroundings, and recommend it to His servants for their use in the stewardship of God's gifts. Scrupulous conscientiousness need not be divorced, as it too frequently is, from ordinary prudence and

[1] Luke xii. 21 : μὴ εἰς θεὸν πλουτῶν.

[2] Luke xii. 15 : οὐκ ἐν τῷ περισσεύειν τινὶ ἡ ζωὴ αὐτοῦ ἐστιν ἐκ τῶν ὑπαρχόντων αὐτῷ.

knowledge of the world; the sons of light should not be less shrewd or well equipped than those who have no higher aim than to promote their own selfish ends. Quite another view of the subject is presented by the parable of the Rich Man and Lazarus, which follows the Rich Fool, and was perhaps spoken on the same occasion.[1] Here it is not the unscrupulous money-grubber who is delineated, but the man who is already in possession of riches inherited or acquired, and spends them upon himself without a thought of the brother who is suffering or starving at his gate. He is seen in two strongly contrasted positions, clad in purple and fine linen and faring sumptuously day by day, and a little after, stripped to the soul, and tormented in the only flame that naked souls can feel. "Father Abraham" (for the man is a Jew) is appealed to in vain; the exchange of the rich man's and the beggar's lots belongs to the justice of things, with which the righteous patriarch would not have interfered if he could. The picture may seem to favour the agitator who advocates the spoliation of the rich, or at

[1] Luke xvi. 19-31.

least may be construed into a denunciation of the greater inequalities of life. But in fact it does not touch any social question; the reversal of social *status* to which it refers takes effect in the future life and not in this. Moreover, the parable does not teach that at death the very rich are necessarily plunged into helpless misery, and the very poor raised to Paradise. The Rich Man suffers because money was his only good, and having lost it he has lost all.[1] Thus the story is not aimed at wealth, or even at the abuse of wealth, but at the selfish thoughtlessness which is one of wealth's chief dangers; it does not help the destructive views of the socialist, though it may well give pause to owners of property who use their money merely for the advancement of personal comfort or display. One more parable may be classed with this group, and it is perhaps the gem of the whole collection. The Good Samaritan,[2] as it seems, is not a rich man; he travels without retinue, and has no beast but the one he

---

[1] Luke xvi. 25 : ἀπέλαβες τὰ ἀγαθά σου. Cf. vi. 24 : οὐαὶ ὑμῖν τοῖς πλουσίοις, ὅτι ἀπέχετε τὴν παράκλησιν ὑμῶν.

[2] Luke x. 30–37.

rides; the two small silver coins [1] which he pulls out of his girdle and leaves with the host do not suggest a well-filled purse. But whatever he has, his money, his beast, his time, is placed at the service of a wounded Jew, who has no claim on his charity beyond the fact that he is a brother-man in need. Thus the Good Samaritan is the exact opposite of the Rich Man who, with abundant means and daily opportunities, passed through life without lifting a finger to relieve distress. Perhaps the old Christian tradition—older than Origen [2]—which saw in the Good Samaritan the Supreme Example of Charity, is not altogether baseless; it is to Himself that the Lord seems in fact to point each of us when He says, "Go and do thou likewise." But the mystical interpretation must not be suffered to eclipse the primary reference of the parable, or its plain lesson as to the duty and privilege of rendering service to suffering humanity, irrespective of kindred or creed.

2. After the parables of St. Luke's Gospel,

[1] Luke x. 35 : ἐκβαλὼν δύο δηνάρια.
[2] Cf. Orig. *Hom. in Luc.* 34.

the reader's attention is arrested by its abundance of epigrammatic sayings, chiefly reminiscences of our Lord's conversation with individuals or small groups of followers. These Lucan sayings, like the Lucan parables, have to do with the mystery of the personal life.

First, there are those which throw light upon the workings of our Lord's own mind and soul. It is noteworthy that we owe to St. Luke the one recorded saying of Christ's childhood, and what was probably the last word spoken on the Cross. There is a close affinity between the two. "I must be in my Father's house"[1] reveals His early consciousness of a Divine Sonship, and the attraction which the Father's Presence possessed for Him even during the immaturity of His human life; "Father, into Thy hands I commend My spirit"[2] testifies to the victory of filial trust and the consummation of filial obedience at the moment of His departure from the world. Other words

---

[1] Luke ii. 49.

[2] Luke xxiii. 46. On the rendering of ἐν τοῖς πατρός μου, see F. Field, *Notes on the Translation of the N.T.* p. 50 f.

dropped in the intervening years reflect the progress of the struggle by which He was perfected. "I beheld Satan fallen as lightning from heaven."[1] "I have a baptism to be baptized with, and how am I straitened till it be finished."[2] "I cast out demons and perform cures to-day and to-morrow, and the third day I am perfected; howbeit I must go on my way to-day and to-morrow and the day following, for it cannot be that a prophet perish out of Jerusalem."[3] "With desire I have desired to eat this passover with you before I suffer; for I say unto you, I will not eat it until it be fulfilled in the Kingdom of God."[4] "That which concerneth Me hath fulfilment."[5] In this catena of Lucan sayings the whole course of the Great Sacrifice can be traced, and what a wealth of spiritual teaching

[1] Luke x. 18.

[2] Luke xii. 50. With ἕως ὅτου τελεσθῇ comp. the final τετέλεσται (John xix. 30).

[3] Luke xiii. 32 f. [4] Luke xxii. 15 f.

[5] Luke xxii. 37 (R.V.); see Field, *ad loc.* If τὸ περὶ ἐμοῦ be taken to mean "My work and life" (cf. xxiv. 27), we may keep the rendering of A.V. "hath an end," the more obvious sense of τέλος ἔχει.

there is here, notwithstanding the obscurity in which the profound thought is partly wrapped, the Christian heart will readily discover for itself.

Only less interesting than these glimpses into the inner life of Christ are the sayings which light up the character or the destiny of His followers. We learn, for instance, from a group of answers [1] to candidates for discipleship the exacting standard which He raised before the eyes of those who would follow Him: " The foxes have holes, and the birds of the air have nests, but the Son of Man hath not where to lay His head "—this to one who had just made an unlimited offer of service ; " Leave the dead to bury their own dead "—this to another who asked for time to pay the last offices of filial duty to his father; " No man having put his hand to the plough, and looking back, is fit for the Kingdom of God "—this to a third, who desired, like Elisha, to bid farewell to his kindred before he embarked on his new calling. In each case the individual character was read, and a test applied which, it cannot

[1] Luke ix. 57 ff.

be doubted, brought to light its weakness or its strength. The enthusiasm of a woman who felicitated the mother of so great a Prophet is directed to a more practical end by the answer: "Yea rather, blessed are they that hear the word of God and keep it."[1] Simon Peter's early shrinking from the awful Presence of One whose mere word filled the nets that a night's toil had left empty, is met by an inspiring call to confidence and to a higher service, "Fear not, from henceforth thou shalt catch men.";[2] while the same Apostle's later excess of confidence is corrected by the plain warning that nothing but the Master's intercession had saved him from the danger which awaited all the disciples of falling like chaff through Satan's sieve and being lost.[3] Other sayings shew how clearly Jesus recognised the elements of the higher life under the most unpromising exterior. In the woman that was a sinner He saw one who "loved much,"[4] and

---

[1] Luke xi. 28.   [2] Luke v. 10.

[3] Luke xxii. 31 : Ὁ Σατανᾶς ἐξῃτήσατο ὑμᾶς τοῦ σινιάσαι ὡς τὸν σῖτον· ἐγὼ δὲ ἐδεήθην περὶ σοῦ.

[4] Luke vii. 47.

whose sins had been forgiven;[1] in Zacchæus, the rich and well-hated chief of the Jericho toll-collectors, He discovered a true son of Abraham, to whose house salvation had come on the day that he welcomed the Lord;[2] in the robber who repented upon the cross, one who that very day would be "in Paradise," and not merely in Abraham's bosom, but in the company of the Christ.[3] Perhaps the most delicate of all these appreciations of character is that which is revealed in the story of Martha and Mary.[4] "Jesus loved Martha and her sister";[5] and His love was returned by both the sisters, but each of them welcomed Him in her own way. Martha, perhaps the responsible hostess, was "distracted about much waiting" at table; Mary took her seat at His feet, listening to His discourse. Perhaps no reference would have been made by the Lord to this characteristic difference had not

[1] Luke vii. 48 (ἀφέωνται).

[2] Luke xix. 2, 9.

[3] Luke xxiii. 43: μετ' ἐμοῦ ἔσῃ ἐν τῷ παραδείσῳ, cf. xvi. 22 f.

[4] Luke x. 38–42.   [5] John xi. 5.

Martha invited it by appealing to Him to bid Mary help her. Then came the verdict: "Martha, Martha, thou art anxious and disturbed about many things, but there is need of few, or of but one;[1] for the good portion is that which Mary hath chosen, and it shall not be taken from her." Both women were serving Him according to their lights, but Mary had judged best what service would possess the greatest value in His eyes. Anxiety about external details, even in the cause of Christ, tends to distract and divide the soul; He asks but for one thing, an undivided heart, possessed by the single desire to know and do His will.[2]

Another group of sayings deals with whole classes of men, but still in reference to personal life and character. Sometimes the Lord seems to recognise but two types of human character and two issues of life, as when on hearing the

[1] Reading with ℵ B L ὀλίγων δέ ἐστιν χρεία ἢ ἑνός.

[2] See the interesting sermons of Augustine on this passage (civ., cv.), especially civ. 5: "Bona sunt ministeria circa pauperes . . . exhortamur ad haec . . . melius est tamen quod elegit Maria . . . a te auferetur aliquando onus necessitatis; aeterna est dulcedo veritatis."

report of Pilate's outrage on certain Galileans He exclaimed, "Except ye repent, ye shall all in like manner perish."[1] Sometimes, on the other hand, there is in His judgements a nice balancing of varying responsibilities and performances, as when we read of the many stripes or the few which await those who neglect to do the will of the Master, according as they "knew" or "knew not" what was expected from them.[2] Much of this teaching is directed against the moral insensibility of an age which was letting slip the greatest opportunity that any generation had enjoyed. "Ye know how to interpret the face of the earth and the heaven; but how is it that ye know not how to interpret this time"?[3] "Were not the ten cleansed? but where are the nine"?[4] "Remember Lot's wife."[5] "If thou hadst known in this day, even thou, the things which belong unto peace! but now they are hid from thine eyes."[6] "Daughters of Jerusalem, weep not for me, but weep for yourselves and for your children; for

---

[1] Luke xiii. 1–3. [2] Luke xii. 47 f.
[3] Luke xii. 56. [4] Luke xvii. 17.
[5] Luke xvii. 32. [6] Luke xix. 42.

PECULIAR TO ST. LUKE 117

if they do these things in the green tree, what shall be done in the dry?"[1] With these words of stern warning or sad foreboding we may contrast the note of hope or triumph now and again sounded when loyal disciples are in view. "Lift up your heads, because your redemption draweth nigh."[2] "I appoint unto you a kingdom, even as My Father appointed unto Me."[3] Or again, the gentleness and love of the assurance to St. Peter, "I made supplication for thee that thy faith fail not";[4] or the prayer for the crucifiers, "Father, forgive them, for they know not what they do."[5] Such words, beyond their original reference, hold teaching and inspiration for all generations of mankind.

It remains to consider what special aspects of Christ's teaching are revealed by the Lucan parables and sayings.

Perhaps the most prominent feature of the Lucan teaching may be best described in a phrase used by St. Luke himself. He represents

---

[1] Luke xxiii. 28 ff.   [2] Luke xxi. 28.
[3] Luke xxii. 29.   [4] Luke xxii. 32.
[5] Luke xxiii. 34. If not a part of St. Luke's original Gospel, this prayer is in keeping with the Lucan sayings.

the people of Nazareth as marvelling at the "words of grace"[1] which came out of the mouth of Jesus. It is the *graciousness* of Christ's utterances in this Gospel which at once impresses every thoughtful reader. The Evangelist has been well called by Dante "scriba mansuetudinis Christi."[2] "A peine est-il une anecdote, une parabole propre à Luc, qui ne respire cet esprit de miséricorde et d'appel aux pécheurs ... L'Évangile de Luc est par excellence l'Évangile du pardon."[3] So writes Ernest Renan, adding, "On voit la parfaite conformité de ces vues avec celles de Paul."[4] The affinity of the Third Gospel to the Epistles of St. Paul was noticed in early times, and Irenæus even regards the Gospel as a record of that which was preached by the Apostle.[5] But St. Paul's Gospel, if we may

[1] Luke iv. 22, ἐθαύμαζον ἐπὶ τοῖςλόγοις τῆς χάριτος κ.τ.λ. Cf. Psa. xliv. (xlv.) 2 cited by Plummer from Origen: ἐξεχύθη ἡ χάρις ἐν χείλεσίν σου.

[2] Cited by Plummer, p. xlii.

[3] *Les Évangiles*, p. 266 f.

[4] *Les Évangiles*, p. 269.

[5] Iren. iii. 1. 1, καὶ Λουκᾶς δέ, ὁ ἀκόλουθος Παύλου, τὸ ὑπ' ἐκείνου κηρυσσόμενον εὐαγγέλιον ἐν βιβλίῳ κατέθετο.

trust his own account of it,[1] was a simple record of the death and resurrection of Jesus Christ; nor can we conceive of him as repeating narratives and sayings of which he could have had but a second-hand knowledge. Still less can the exquisite parables and utterances of the Gospel according to St. Luke have proceeded from the imagination of St. Paul. His genius lay in other directions; he was master of close argument and passionate appeal, and no one could paint an ideal in more glowing colours, but for a creation such as the parable of the Good Samaritan he shews no capacity. So far as Paulinism is to be found in the Lucan teaching, it may be claimed as an original element in Christianity, due to the Master Himself. It is Christ and not St. Paul who speaks to us in the Third Gospel; and if the words often seem to savour of Pauline doctrine, it is because St. Paul above all other men of his time assimilated that side of our Lord's teaching which this Gospel has specially preserved. It is perhaps too much to say with Harnack that Paul was "the one who under-

[1] 1 Cor. xv. 1 ff.

stood the Master, and continued His work"; [1] but at any rate it was given to him in an especial degree to emphasize the element in the Master's teaching which sets forth the mystery of the Divine Grace. And it is the Divine Grace which is the keynote of the Lucan teaching. Not that in the teaching of Christ, as St. Luke records it, there is any formal doctrine of Grace, any discussion or dogmatic statement such as finds a place in the Epistles of St. Paul. In the Gospel the teaching upon this subject is concrete; it is brought into line with the facts of life, exemplified in the experience of man. "To-day hath this Scripture been fulfilled in your ears"; [2] "her sins, which are many, are forgiven, for she loved much"; [3] "this man went down to his house justified rather than the other"; [4] "to-day is salvation come to this house, forasmuch as he also is a son of Abraham." [5] These are examples of the personal form which the Lord's teaching upon

[1] *Das Wesen des Christentums*, p. 110 (E. Tr. p. 176).
[2] Luke iv. 21.
[3] Luke vii. 47.
[4] Luke xviii. 14.
[5] Luke xix. 9.

the subject of Grace always takes. He is the Physician dispensing remedies, and not the professor teaching their use. His purpose is not to expound their nature or the laws by which they operate, or to urge their employment, but to heal and save by their means. Consequently the Gospel of St. Luke touches thousands to whom the Pauline Epistles are almost a sealed book. The words of the Master are a text which he that runs may read; the writings of the disciple are a commentary upon the text, and not the primary source.

The graciousness of the Lucan teaching is not untempered by a just severity. The sermon at Nazareth which began with "words of grace" ended with a reproof that filled the synagogue with indignation.[1] In St. Matthew the Sermon on the Mount begins with beatitudes only; in St. Luke the beatitudes are balanced by woes.[2] It is St. Luke who calls attention to the double warning against impenitence,[3] the doom of the barren fig-tree,[4] the hopeless misery which follows neglect of

[1] Luke iv. 23 ff.
[2] Luke vi. 24-26.
[3] Luke xiii. 3 and 5.
[4] Luke xiii. 9.

the opportunities of life,[1] the fate of those who will not have their true King to reign over them [2] the terrors of the coming end.[3] There is a sternness even toward disciples which marks this Gospel: witness the rebuke administered to James and John;[4] the discouraging words addressed to the three who purposed to follow Christ;[5] the uncompromising demand for vigilance and service made upon those who had already enlisted ;[6] the charge of folly and unbelief laid against the two who were overtaken by the risen Lord on the way to Emmaus.[7] In all this we see tokens of a love which is unsparing because it is just and true, an $\dot{\alpha}\pi o\tau o\mu i\alpha$ which is consistent with the highest $\chi\rho\eta\sigma\tau\acute{o}\tau\eta\varsigma$.[8] Of the easy good-nature that shrinks from the pain of rebuking sin or warning against failure there is no trace. The "grace of our Lord Jesus Christ," as it is set forth in this Gospel, does not exclude but rather implies a "wrath of the Lamb"[9] which is the complement of His mercy.

[1] Luke xvi. 24 ff.
[2] Luke xix. 27.
[3] Luke xxiii. 29–31.
[4] Luke ix. 55.
[5] Luke ix. 57 ff.
[6] Luke xii. 35 ff.
[7] Luke xxiv. 25.
[8] Rom. xi. 22.
[9] Apoc. vi. 17.

PECULIAR TO ST. LUKE

Neither of these features of Christ's teaching is wholly absent from the other Synoptic Gospels, but in St. Luke both are prominent. Still, the first may be said to be the prevalent note of the Lucan teaching. If in St. Mark our Lord appears in the character of the Evangelist of the Kingdom of God, and in St. Matthew as the Legislator of the Kingdom, in St. Luke He reveals Himself as the Physician, the Redeemer, and the supreme Master of mankind.

THE TEACHING IN THE GOSPEL OF ST. JOHN

CHAPTER V

THE TEACHING IN THE GOSPEL OF ST JOHN

IT has recently been maintained [1] that while the discourses of the Fourth Gospel are trustworthy as a whole, and due to the Apostle John, the narrative is for the most part the work of a member of the School of St. John whose purpose was to supply an historical framework for the discourses, and who did not hesitate here and there to imagine the events which he describes.

The theory is ingenious rather than convincing.[2] Most readers will feel that whether

---

[1] By Dr. H. H. Wendt (*Das Johannes-Evangelium*, Göttingen, 1900: E. Tr., Edinburgh, 1902).

[2] It is briefly but adequately answered by Dr. Lock, in the *Journal of Theological Studies*, iv. 2, p. 194 ff.

St. John is to be regarded as the writer or not, the Gospel which bears his name is a unity which cannot be satisfactorily distributed between two authors. But the attempt to do so will not have been without value if it calls attention to the subsidiary character of the Johannine narrative. The Synoptists are primarily historians or biographers; the writer of the Fourth Gospel regards history or biography as subservient to direct instruction. He has given us what is pre-eminently the Gospel of the Teaching of Christ.

Yet St. John's narrative stands always in close relation to the didactic element in his book. It gives point and reality to the discourses, which owe to it more than the reader may at first suppose. Happily the Evangelist has been able in every instance to recover the occasion upon which the teaching was given, or the circumstances out of which it arose. A mere collection of "Logia" would not merely have missed the literary charm which belongs to this Gospel; it would have been intrinsically less valuable. How much the narrative contributes to the right understanding of the teaching will be evident if the reader tries to imagine any one of the great discourses divorced from its context; if, *e.g.*, he separates the discourse of chapter v. from the Sabbath miracle which preceded it, or the teaching of chapter vi. from the miracle of the Loaves, or the pastoral imagery of chapter x. from the incidents of chapter ix.; or if he lose sight of the occasion of the farewell discourse in chapters xiv.–xvi. Moreover, the Gospel of St. John is rich in conversations which are of no less importance than the discourses, and in these the teaching gains immeasurably in interest and power from the dramatic form in which it is cast. It would no doubt have been possible to convey the instruction of chapters iii. and iv. by means of excerpts, or in a continuous form; but at what a sacrifice of strength, and even of momentous truth!

The narrative, however, serves a further purpose. It explains to a great extent the special character of the Johannine teaching. With the exception of the teaching upon the Bread of Life, the whole of the public discourses in this Gospel and nearly all the conversations belong to the Judæan Ministry.[1] But the social and religious atmosphere of Judæa and especially of Jerusalem, where most of the Judæan teaching was given, differed widely from that of Galilee; and if due allowance be made for this change of circumstances, it will go far to account for the new form in which the teaching is cast. There are other considerations which must not be overlooked, such as the greater capacity for assimilating the profounder truths that fell from the Master's lips which may reasonably be ascribed to St. John; but apart from these, it is natural to suppose that the deeper teaching was given with greater freedom at Jerusalem than at Capernaum, in the Temple precinct and in the hearing of the cultured and responsible people who made Solomon's Porch or the Treasury their place of resort[2] than to the peasants, fishermen, toll-gatherers, and motley crowd of followers who thronged the Lord's

---

[1] Only in John ii. 1–12, iv. 43–54, vi., vii. 1–9, is the scene laid in Galilee; iv. 5–42 belongs to Samaria, and x. 40–xi. 16 to Peræa.

[2] John viii. 20, x. 23.

daily progress along the shore of the northern lake.

All this might be worked out at some length, but our space forbids, and we must hasten to glance at the subject-matter of the Johannine teaching. It falls roughly under two heads. It is a self-revelation, in which the Lord unfolds to the Jews,[1] and yet more fully to the Twelve, the mystery of His own Person, mission, and work. It is also a revelation of the mystery of the spiritual life which characterizes the subjects of the Kingdom of God. Neither of these topics is absent from the Synoptic teaching, but in the conversations and discourses of the Fourth Gospel they are treated on a larger scale and exhibited in new lights.

1. In His self-revelation our Lord manifests some measure of the same reserve which we have noticed in the Synoptic Gospels. Though at Jerusalem men were freely discussing the possibility that Jesus was the Christ,[2] the

[1] On the meaning to be given to οἱ 'Ιουδαῖοι in this Gospel see Westcott, *St. John*, p. ix.

[2] Cp. John vii. 26 ff., ix. 22.

Lord appears not to have expressly claimed the title, even if His words implied that it belonged to Him.[1] Moreover, at Jerusalem, as at Capernaum, He called Himself "the Son of Man," though perhaps not so frequently.[2] On the other hand, the public discourses of the Fourth Gospel are full of language which goes beyond any claim of Messiahship, as the Jews understood that office. Of these self-manifestations the most remarkable are those which occur in the discourses of chapters v., viii., and x., all of which were delivered to hostile audiences,[3] and the second and the third (at least in part) within the precinct.[4] It was under such circumstances that Jesus spoke as follows: "My Father worketh even until now, and I work." "What things soever He doeth, these

[1] John x. 24 f.: εἰπὸν ἡμῖν παρρησίᾳ . . . εἶπον ὑμῖν καὶ οὐ πιστεύετε, cf. viii. 25. The only express statement seems to have been made to the Samaritan woman (iv. 26).

[2] The title occurs only in i. 51, iii. 13 f., viii. 28, ix. 35 (אBD), xii. 23 (cf. 24), xiii. 31.

[3] See v. 16, viii. 59, x. 31, 39. The "believing" Jews of ch. viii. 20 are scarcely an exception.

[4] John viii. 59, x. 23.

IN THE GOSPEL OF ST. JOHN

the Son also doeth in like manner." "As the Father raiseth the dead and quickeneth them, even so the Son quickeneth whom He will; for neither doth the Father judge any man, but He hath given all judgement unto the Son, that all may honour the Son even as they honour the Father." "For as the Father hath life in Himself, even so gave He to the Son also to have life in Himself."[1] "I am from above, I am not of this world." "Except ye believe that I am He, ye shall die in your sins." "As the Father taught Me, I speak these things." "I do always the things that are pleasing to Him." "I came forth, and am come from God." "Before Abraham was (γενέσθαι), I am (εἰμί)."[2] "I and the Father are one (ἕν ἐσμεν)." "The Father is in Me, and I in the Father."[3]

It is not surprising that the Jews of Jerusalem were in some cases bewildered, in others scandalized, by these extraordinary claims. Some asked, "Where is Thy father?"

[1] John v. 17, 19, 21 ff., 26.
[2] John viii. 23 f., 28, 42, 58.
[3] John x. 30, 38.

"who art Thou?" "whom makest Thou Thyself?"[1] Others saw quite clearly what Jesus meant; He "called God His own (ἴδιον) Father, making Himself equal with God"; "Thou, being a man," they said bluntly, "makest Thyself God."[2] On two occasions this conviction lashed them into a fury; they seized the fragments of marble which were lying on the pavement of the courts, and would have stoned Him for a blasphemer then and there.[3]

Were they mistaken in their interpretation of His words? A large and growing body of modern theologians is of opinion that they were. The question is a vital one. Jesus taught as He did at the risk of His life, and must therefore have regarded this element in His teaching as of primary importance. That it was reserved for Jerusalem and for the Temple invests it with especial solemnity.

What then is the nature of the Sonship which our Lord claims in these discourses? Is it merely an ethical relation to God, a relation

[1] John viii. 19, 25, 53.
[2] John v. 18, x. 33.
[3] John viii. 59, x. 31.

of love and trust and intimate fellowship, unique in its perfection, but the same in kind as that which belongs to all living members of His Church? Or is it, over and above this, an essential relation, involving a participation in the inner life of God? In support of the former view it is argued that in other passages the Lord attributes to the disciples the same distinctive features of Divine Sonship: "They are not of the world, even as I am not of the world"; "the glory which Thou hast given Me I have given unto them, that they may be one, even as We are One."[1] Such words shew clearly that there is an analogy between the Sonship of Christ and the sonship of believers; the latter is, if we may dare to speak so, modelled upon the former; the ethical characteristics of the two differ only in degree. But the question before us is not answered by pointing out certain resemblances. Can we apply to the disciples of Christ, in any state of perfection which can be reached by a created nature, *all* that the Lord has claimed for Himself? Can they be said, *e.g.*, to have life

[1] John xvii. 16, 22.

in themselves *as the Father hath life in Himself?*[1] Would any degree of moral assimilation to God justify a merely human being in saying, "I and the Father are one"? In nearly every one of our Lord's sayings about His Sonship there is something which cannot be transferred to His disciples, which the Christian consciousness refuses to regard as applicable to itself. Thus His words justify the Evangelist's deduction that He is "the Only-begotten Son," and even "God only-begotten." It is not without significance that the writer of the Fourth Gospel does not permit himself to call believers "sons of God"; they are "children," τέκνα θεοῦ,[2] but he reserves the title ὁ υἱὸς τοῦ θεοῦ for our Lord.

On one occasion, indeed, Jesus seems to deprecate the logical import of His words. "Is it not written in your Law, 'I said, Ye are gods'? If He called them 'gods' unto whom

[1] There is a sense in which believers may be said ζωὴν ἔχειν ἐν ἑαυτοῖς (cf. John vi. 53), but not ὥσπερ ὁ πατήρ (v. 26).

[2] Cf. John i. 12, xi. 52; 1 John iii. 1 f., 10, v. 2. Τέκνον is used by St. John of our Lord only in Apoc. xii. 4 f., where His human birth is in view.

the word of God came, and the Scripture cannot be broken, say ye of Him whom the Father sanctified and sent into the world, 'Thou blasphemest,' because I said 'I am the Son of God'?"[1] The argument is from the less to the greater: 'if Divinity could be ascribed by an inspired writer to mere mortal men who were entrusted with the Divine word in the ordinary way, how can it be denied to One who has been sent from God with a direct message to mankind?' Our Lord purposely limits Himself here to the lowest view which could be taken of His mission; even on that hypothesis He has the right to call Himself Son of God. But it is clear that He does this without prejudice to any higher claim, and His words cannot be taken to neutralize all that He has elsewhere said as to His essential oneness with the Father.

It is, however, to the farewell discourses of chapters xiv.–xvi., and the last prayer of Jesus in chapter xvii., that we must look for the crown-

[1] John x. 34 ff. Cf. Ps. lxxxii. 6 f. (LXX.: ἐγὼ εἶπα Θεοί ἐστε, καὶ υἱοὶ Ὑψίστου πάντες· ὑμεῖς δὲ δὴ ὡς ἄνθρωποι ἀποθνήσκετε).

ing self-manifestation of the Only-begotten Son. Here the atmosphere is entirely changed; the Lord is no longer bearing witness to Himself before a hostile and menacing crowd, but taking the Twelve into His confidence,[1] or engaged in intimate communion with God. We are admitted into the sanctuary of the Master's spirit, and we see His Divine Sonship asserting itself both in His relations with the disciples and in His intercourse with the Father. "Believe on (εἰς) God," He says to the Twelve, "and believe also on (εἰς) Me." "He that hath seen Me hath seen the Father." "If a man love Me . . . My Father will love him, and We will come unto him and make Our abode with him."[2] "I will send [the Comforter] unto you from the Father."[3] "He shall glorify Me, for He shall take of Mine and shall declare it unto you; all things whatsoever the Father hath are Mine."[4] "The Father Himself loveth you, because ye have loved Me, and have believed that I came forth from (παρά) the Father." "I came out from (ἐκ) the Father, and am come

---

[1] Cf. John xv. 15.
[2] John xiv. 1, 9, 23.
[3] John xv. 26, xvi. 7.
[4] John xvi. 14 f., cf. xvii. 9

into the world; again, I leave the world, and go unto the Father."[1] He prays: "O Father, glorify Thou Me with Thine own self with the glory which I had with Thee before the world was." "Father, that which Thou hast given Me, I will that where I am they also may be with Me, that they may behold My glory which Thou hast given Me; for Thou lovedst Me before the foundation of the world."[2] It is right to set against this language one or two sentences which seem to point in an opposite direction, such as: "The Father is greater than I;" "this is life eternal, that they should know Thee, the only true God, and Him whom Thou didst send, even Jesus Christ."[3] But even these passages, however they may be interpreted, assign to Jesus an unique position in the order of being. Who is this person who ventures to compare Himself with the Father, and coordinates Himself with the only true God, as one whom it is necessary to know in order to have eternal life? Nor do these statements

[1] John xvi. 27 f.
[2] John xvii. 5, 24.
[3] John xiv. 28, xvii. 3.

really contravene the rest of the teaching. The superior greatness of the Father [1] is wholly consistent with our Lord's repeated attribution of His glory and His very being to the Father's gift; the title "only true God" does not exclude from Godhead the Son, who is one with the Father. The Christology of the Fourth Gospel is as truly monotheistic [2] as that of the Synoptists, though it recognises more distinctly that in the Divine Unity there is a plurality of essential relations.

The Johannine teaching is not less full in reference to the mission and work of Christ. Our Lord constantly speaks of Himself as sent and commissioned [3] by the Father. The work of His life was to do the will of the Person who

---

[1] On the interpretation of John xiv. 28 see the additional note in Westcott.

[2] Cf. John v. 44, where again monotheism asserts itself in a discourse which claims Divine honour for the Son.

[3] Πέμπειν is used in John iv. 34; v. 23 f., 30, 37; vi. 38 f., 44; vii. 16, 18, 28, 33; ix. 4; xii. 44 f., 49; xiii. 20; xiv. 24; xv. 21; xvi. 5; ἀποστέλλειν in iii. 17, 34; v. 36, 38; vi. 29, 57; vii. 29; viii. 42; x. 36; xi. 42; xvii. 3, 8, 18, 21, 23, 25; xx. 21. The two words are discussed by Westcott (additional note on xx. 21).

sent Him;[1] His words and His acts were spoken and performed in the name of God.[2] From one point of view the end of His mission was to bear witness to the truth;[3] from another, it was to save the world, to give eternal life to men.[4] But these two aspects of His work are one in fact, since the truth is a saving power, liberating men from sin and death.[5] The mission of Christ would end with His return to the Father, but it was to be followed or rather continued by a mission of the Spirit. Beyond this again Jesus foresaw a general resurrection and judgement, in both of which He was to take the principal part.[6] There are, in short, no bounds to the powers which He claims in the domain of both flesh and spirit. "I am the Light of the world;" "I am the Resurrection and the Life;" "I am the Way, and the Truth, and the Life; no one cometh unto the Father

[1] John iv. 34; vi. 38; ix. 4; xii. 49.
[2] John v. 36; viii. 28 f.; xii. 49.
[3] John xviii. 37.
[4] John iii. 16 f.; x. 10; xvii. 2 f.
[5] John viii. 32 ff.; 52.
[6] John v. 21 ff.

but by Me."[1] These words, it is evident, extend further than the brief earthly ministry; they point to vast influences permeating all human history and that which lies beyond it; they reveal in dim outline a work which is now in course of fulfilment and stretches forth into the infinite future.

Such teaching dazzles by its splendour. But if it is difficult to imagine it as proceeding from human lips, still less can we believe that it originated in the mind of the Evangelist. Even a St. John was incapable of such a creation. No adequate explanation of it can be found but that which the Evangelist himself has given. "The Word was God . . . in Him was life and the life was the light of men . . . and the Word became flesh and dwelt among us, and we beheld His glory, glory as of the Only-begotten from the Father (or, as of an only-begotten from a father, ὡς μονογενοῦς παρὰ πατρός)—full of grace and truth."[2]

2. By the side of this great revelation of the Lord's Person and work, and in close connexion

[1] John viii. 22; xi. 25; xiv. 6.
[2] John i. 1–14.

with it, the Fourth Gospel places another, the revelation of the Divine life in the subjects of the Kingdom of God.

Three classical passages [1] deal with this second mystery—the conversation with Nicodemus, the conversation with the Samaritan woman, and the conversation and discourse at Capernaum.

There is a remarkable contrast in the situations represented in the first and second of these interviews. In the first our Lord is seen in conference with a Pharisee, who is also a member of the Sanhedrin;[2] in the second He converses with a woman who is not of pure Israelite blood, and whose Bible contained only the Pentateuch. One of these persons was an inquirer, the other thoughtless, and disposed to be captious. Both receive instructions according to their separate capacities, and it is interesting to study the great Master's treatment of each case, as well as the teaching itself. To Nicodemus, a "teacher of Israel," the Lord speaks of the mystery of the New Birth. He

[1] John iii., iv., vi.
[2] John iii. 1; cf. vii. 50.

who would "see" or "enter into" the Kingdom of God must be "born from above."[1] Life in a Divine Kingdom must have a supramundane source. In the Synoptic Gospels the Kingdom is viewed chiefly in its outward and visible results, as it affects conduct; here for the first time the spiritual life which lies behind conduct is revealed in its genesis and growth. Spirit can be generated only by spirit. But spirit is invisible; the wind, its nearest analogue, which both in Aramaic and Greek shares its name (רוּחָא, πνεῦμα), can be heard but not seen as it sweeps along with irresistible force; in like manner the spiritual life eludes observation, and yet works the greatest wonders in the world. For spiritual life and spiritual birth, though from above, are enacted on earth (ἐπίγεια),[2] and are not transcendental conceptions, but facts of daily experience. Finally, Jesus connects this revelation with His own person and mission, and with the ultimate purpose of His coming.

---

[1] So on the whole it seems best to render ἄνωθεν in iii. 3, 7; cf. iii. 31, ὁ ἄνωθεν ἐρχόμενος, and xix. 11, δεδομένον ἄνωθεν; also James i. 17, iii. 17 ἡ ἄνωθεν σοφία.

[2] John iii. 12.

IN THE GOSPEL OF ST. JOHN 145

"We speak that we do know;" "no man hath ascended into heaven but He that descended out of heaven, even the Son of Man;"[1] "the Son of Man must be lifted up, that whosoever believeth may in Him have eternal life."[2]

With the Samaritan woman another course is pursued. The Teacher starts with the scene which lay before Him. He "sat by the well," the gift of the patriarch Jacob,[3] from which for centuries daily supplies of water had been laboriously drawn.[4] In contrast with this earthly source of refreshment, He places the Gift of God,[5] and its store of "living water," which not only quenches thirst at the moment but becomes a spring of inward life.[6] In this teaching less emphasis is laid on the beginnings of the new life and on its mysterious nature and powers, and more on its source, course, and issue. It is the gift of Christ, Himself

---

[1] The words ὁ ὢν ἐν τῷ οὐρανῷ (ΑΓΠ), etc., are "Western and Syrian," and should probably be omitted; see WH., *Notes*, p. 75.

[2] John iii. 13, 15. [3] John iv. 6.
[4] John iv. 11, 15. [5] John iv. 10; cf. iii. 16.
[6] John iv. 23.

the Gift of God. It enters into man's nature, satisfies his deepest desires, and becomes within him a spring of life, ever sending fresh rills of life through his being till it ends in life everlasting. No direct mention is made here of the spiritual nature of this new life; yet the conversation does not end without a reference to this point. "God is Spirit, and they that worship Him must worship Him in spirit and in truth." The water of life is the supply of the Spirit of Christ, as we learn from a later chapter,[1] and as the conversation with Nicodemus has already suggested.[2]

In the Synoptic Gospels the first miracle of the Loaves is not the occasion of any teaching beyond a few remarks addressed to the Twelve.[3] But in the Fourth Gospel it leads to a series of conversations and discourses scarcely surpassed in importance by any other. We have first a conversation with the people who had crossed from the scene of the miracle to seek Jesus at Capernaum;[4] then a formal

---

[1] John vii. 37 ff.; cf. Apoc. vii. 17; xxii. 1, 17.
[2] John iii. 5, ἐξ ὕδατος καὶ πνεύματος.
[3] Mark viii. 14 ff.   [4] John vi. 26–40.

reply to "the Jews," delivered in part or in whole in the Capernaum synagogue;[1] and lastly, a few words of explanation addressed to His own disciples. In the conversation with the ignorant people from Bethsaida our Lord simply reveals Himself as "the Bread of Life," in reference to the recent miracle; in His answer to the Jews He speaks of this Bread as consisting of His Flesh and Blood; while to His disciples He gives a key to the enigmas He had uttered. The teaching is briefly as follows:—The spiritual life requires spiritual food. Jesus is Himself this food; not, however, in His pre-existent life with God, but as the Word made Flesh and giving His flesh for the life of the world. The Incarnation and the Sacrifice are the sustenance of the spiritual man, who through them receives the life which is in Christ. The process is wholly spiritual, for in the things of the spirit the fleshly is of no avail. The words of Christ must therefore be carried into the region of the spiritual and unseen, though they are not on that account of less vital significance. They set

[1] John vi. 43-51, 53-58.

forth the effects which His Manhood and His Death, when spiritually assimilated, exert upon our humanity, strengthening and refreshing the soul, renewing its wasted tissues, and preserving both soul and body to the life everlasting.[1]

But it is to the farewell discourse of chapters xiv.–xvi. that we must look for fuller light upon the mystery of the spiritual life, just as we sought there for our Lord's clearest self-revelation. In this great discourse He deals with men who already knew by experience the power of the new life, so far as it was possible to know it before the actual coming of the Paraclete.[2] To them He was able to speak more fully than to "those who were without." In the earlier chapters two

---

[1] There is a striking correspondence between the spiritual facts taught in John iii., vi., and the two great Sacraments of the Gospel; and this may well have been in the mind of Christ when He spoke. But a sound exegesis will refuse to find a *primary* reference to the Sacraments in words addressed to Jewish hearers before the institution of either rite.

[2] See John xiv. 17, ὑμεῖς γινώσκετε αὐτό, ὅτι παρ' ὑμῖν μένει καὶ ἐν ὑμῖν ἐστιν (BD*: ἔσται ℵAD²L).

great facts of the spiritual life have come into sight. It is spiritual in its nature, and it is the gift of Jesus Christ. These principles are still paramount in the last discourse, but they are seen there in new lights. The personal Spirit of God is at length disclosed as the Agent of spiritual life. When the "Other Paraclete" has come, He will teach the disciples all things, guide them into all the truth, remind them of the teaching of Christ, testify of Christ and glorify Him by interpreting His Person and work.[1] Upon the world the coming of the Spirit will have another effect. The world cannot receive Him, since it has no capacity for spiritual things,[2] yet it will feel His power without knowing whence it comes: convictions will be forced upon it which will change its attitude towards Christ and the Kingdom of God.[3] It may be said that all this refers rather to the mission which the Apostles would find themselves called to fulfil shortly after the Ascension and the Pentecost, than to the mystery of the life of the Spirit in the individual. Certainly

[1] John xiv. 26; xv. 26; xvi. 13 ff.
[2] John xiv. 17.   [3] John xvi. 8.

our Lord does not describe the spiritual experience of ordinary believers, as it is described in the Epistles of St. Paul; for His teaching, far-reaching as its principles are, deals with the persons and circumstances which were immediately before Him. But His words about the Paraclete reveal, so far as it could be revealed at the time, a coming dispensation of the Spirit; and thus they supplement the teaching of the earlier chapters of this Gospel. They make known the existence of a Divine Person, proceeding from the Father and to be sent by the Son, whose very name suggests that He is the Principle of all spiritual life and power.

Yet these chapters which foretell the work of the Paraclete shew no tendency to retract the claims which Jesus had Himself made upon the human spirit. As a matter of fact they repeat those claims, and even reinforce them. The last discourse begins with the command, "Believe on Me," and ends with the cry of triumph, "Be of good cheer, I have overcome the world."[1] Christ's Person and Christ's

[1] John xiv. 1, xvi. 33.

victory are the basis on which the entire fabric of the Christian life is to rest. The life itself is to be one of sustained fellowship with the Master, and absolute loyalty to His commands. "Abide in Me and I in you ... apart from Me ye can do nothing." "If ye keep My commandments ye shall abide in My love ... ye are my friends, if ye do the things which I command you."[1] There is to be no transference from the old life of obedience to Christ to the new life in the Spirit; the latter is but the maturity of the former; the conditions are changed, but the continuity is unbroken. The Spirit does not come to supersede the Son, but to glorify Him.[2] The fulfilment of these words is seen in the heightened Christology of the Epistles, and in this very Gospel, perhaps the last gift of the Apostolic age to the future Church. It is seen in the whole history of the Church, and in the history of every Christian life. Both the Church and the individual are fruitful in proportion as they are loyal to Christ, and to His conception of His own Person and work. The spiritual life can flourish under

[1] John xv. 4 f., 10, 14.   [2] John xv. 14.

no other conditions than those which were imposed upon it by Christ. It is not the Spirit of Christ which leads men to lower Christ's own estimate of His claims, or to minimize the terms of His self-revelation; and there is reason to fear that in proportion as such a tendency grows amongst us, there will be a falling off in the yield of the fruits of the Spirit, which are the *raison d'être* of the Christian Church.

Nothing in this wonderful book is more remarkable than its constant reference to faith in Jesus Christ as the basis of all spiritual life. It is not simply belief in the teaching of Christ on which St. John lays emphasis, but belief on Christ Himself, as the personal object of trust and self-surrender. Πιστεύειν followed by εἰς is a favourite construction with St. John, and in reporting the sayings of Christ he may sometimes have used it rather from force of habit than with any settled purpose; but it certainly conveys an impression distinct in kind from that which is created by the same verb followed by a simple dative, implying trust in the person and not simply in

IN THE GOSPEL OF ST. JOHN

the word of the object of faith.[1] This impression is confirmed in many cases by the context in which the phrase occurs, as *e.g.*, by the coordination in chapter xiv. 1 of trust in Jesus with trust in God. The whole drift of the discourse as well as of the Evangelist's comments is to make personal faith in our Lord the primary condition of salvation. "This is the will of My Father, that every one that beholdeth the Son and believeth on Him should have eternal life."[2] "He that believeth on Me, though he die, yet shall he live, and whosoever liveth and believeth on Me shall never die."[3] "I am come a light into the world, that whosoever believeth on Me may not abide

---

[1] The construction πιστεύειν τινί or τῷ λόγῳ τινός occurs in John ii. 22, iv. 21, 50, v. 24, 38, 46 f., vi. 30, viii. 31, 45 f., x. 37 f., xiv. 11 ; πιστεύειν εἰς τινά or εἰς τὸ ὄεομά τινος in i. 12, ii. 11, 23, iii. 16, 18, 36, iv. 39, vi. 29, *35*, *40*, vii. 5, 31, *38*, 39, 48, viii. 30, ix. *35*, 36, x. 42, xi. *25*, 26, 45, 48, xii. 11, *36*, *37*, 42, *44*, 46, xiv. *1*, *12*, xvi. *9*, xvii. 20 (the sloping numerals represent verses in which Christ is the speaker). Πιστεύειν εἰς is not used in the LXX. even as the equivalent of בְּ הֶאֱמִין; in the Synoptic Gospels it occurs only in Matt. xviii. 6 ; even in St. Paul it is rare. On the other hand it is used in 1 John v. 10, 13.

[2] John vi. 40.   [3] John xi. 25 f.

in the darkness."[1] "The Comforter . . . when He is come, will convict the world in respect of sin, because they believe not in Me."[2] It is idle to say, as Wendt does,[3] that "Jesus only takes account of His own person as the medium of the preaching of the Kingdom of God;" or that "what He regards as the condition of attaining salvation is only the trustful reception of the salvation preached by Him." If it were so, much of His teaching would defeat its own object. The devotion to His person which He demands in all the accounts of the ministry, and which in the Fourth Gospel is characterized as "believing on Him," differs widely from a mere acceptance of His message, however unquestioning and sincere. He requires men to believe His words, but He requires them also to confide wholly in Himself, as the Only-begotten Son of God.

This chapter began with the remark that the Fourth Gospel is preeminently the Gospel of Teaching. It is not less con-

[1] John xii. 46.   [2] John xvi. 9.
[3] *Teaching of Jesus*, E. Tr., ii. p. 309.

IN THE GOSPEL OF ST. JOHN 155

spicuously the Gospel of Faith. We are accustomed to speak of St. John as the Apostle of Love, and the note of love is repeatedly struck in his Gospel [1] as well as in his Epistles. But the note of faith is heard even more distinctly, both in the teaching of our Lord and in the comments of the Evangelist. St. Luke wrote his Gospel in order that Theophilus might know the certainty of the things which he had been taught.[2] St. John's purpose is not less plainly announced: "These are written that ye may believe that Jesus is the Christ, the Son of God, and that believing ye may have life in His name."[3] It is his aim to create in his readers a faith which issues in a life—a faith on the Divine Son, a life in the Spirit which they that believe on Him receive.

[1] *E.g.*, John iii. 16, xiii. 34 f., xiv. 21 ff., xv. 9 ff., 12 f., 17, xvii. 23 ff., xxi. 15 ff.
[2] Luke i. 4.
[3] John xx. 31.

THE TEACHING CONSIDERED AS A WHOLE

CHAPTER VI

THE TEACHING CONSIDERED AS A WHOLE

WE have now taken the evidence of the Four Gospels severally in reference to the Teaching of our Lord. Each Gospel has yielded its special contribution to the great subject, and has impressed upon us its characteristic view. It remains in this last chapter to collect the results, without regard to the sources from which they have been obtained.

Irenæus, in a well-known passage, represents the Gospels as a "quadriform" unity; a single Gospel, presenting four aspects of the One Incarnate Life.[1]

This conception expresses a spiritual fact.

---

[1] Iren. iii. 11. 8, ὁ τῶν ἁπάντων τεχνίτης λόγος . . . ἔδωκεν ἡμῖν τετράμορφον τὸ εὐαγγέλιον, ἑνὶ δὲ πνεύματι συνεχόμενον.

When we compare the Synoptic Gospels with one another, and their united testimony with that of the Fourth Gospel, we become conscious that, notwithstanding wide differences of matter and treatment, the Four are fundamentally agreed in their portrait of the Master and their presentation of His teaching. The same Teacher speaks in all. This conviction justifies us in combining their evidence for the purpose of gaining a general view; indeed, such a process is a necessary complement to the separate examination of the documents.

1. Our Lord began His Galilean ministry by announcing that the Kingdom of God was at hand.[1] This idea was at once the starting-point of His teaching and its basal truth. The term is nearly limited to the Synoptists, and possibly it was not used by Jesus in His public preaching except in Galilee;[2] but the conception meets us everywhere.

[1] Mark i. 15; Matt. iv. 17.
[2] In St. John it occurs only in the conversation with Nicodemus (iii. 3, 15).

AS A WHOLE

The term itself was not new,[1] but the conception was transfigured under the hand of Christ, and its full contents were revealed for the first time. The faith of the Psalmists and Prophets had pictured to itself the Almighty Ruler of the world as seated on His throne in the highest heaven, and from thence directing and controlling the universe. So far as the Divine Kingdom had its seat on earth, it was located at Jerusalem, and its representative was the reigning king of the Davidic line, or, when that line ceased, the expected Messiah. Jesus did not disturb these convictions, which indeed embodied substantial truth. But the Christian idea rises far above them. As Christ preached it, the Kingdom of Heaven is not a territorial empire, whether limited to the land of Israel or co-extensive with the world, but a personal reign, the rule and sway of God over the hearts and lives of men. This Kingdom of God is

---

[1] For examples of its use in pre-Christian Jewish literature see *Ps. Sol.* xvii. 4, ἡ βασιλεία τοῦ θεοῦ ἡμῶν. *Orac. Sibyll.*, iii. 47, βασιλεία μεγίστη ἀθανάτου βασιλῆος ἐπ' ἀνθρώποισι φανεῖσα. For its use in the Targums cf. Deissmann, *Words of Jesus*, p. 91 ff.

162 TEACHING OF OUR LORD

not "here" or "there"; it has no local centre; its seat is in the inner man.[1] It finds its expression in character and life. Its practical results may be learned from the Beatitudes which stand on the threshold of Christ's New Law. They propound the paradox of the Christian life — the blessedness of spiritual poverty and sorrow, of self-forgetfulness and self-dissatisfaction; they exalt into the first rank of virtues the mercy, the purity of heart, the labouring for peace, which reflect the character of God.[2] As the Sermon proceeds, it reveals the new attitude towards God upon which this life rests: an attitude which brings a constant sense of His presence, a firm trust in His love, submission to His will, desire of His approval, imitation of His perfections.[3] To live thus is to reverse the general aims and conduct of mankind; the man who would enter the Kingdom, or even discern its true nature, must be born from above, of water and the Spirit, since only that which is born of the Spirit is spirit, *i.e.*, possesses an affinity

[1] Luke xvii. 21.   Matt. v. 1–9.
[3] Matt. v. 45, 46, vi. 1, 4, 6, 19, 25 ff, vii. 11.

to the spiritual nature of God or a capacity for spiritual truth.[1]

While the Kingdom of God, as it was taught by our Lord, is primarily the present exercise of the Divine sway over hearts dominated by the Spirit, He looks forward to the extension of this spiritual reign until it has covered the earth with subjects of the Kingdom, and issues in a sinless life of unimaginable glory in the presence of God. Thus He teaches His disciples to pray, "Thy Kingdom come," although they had already received the Kingdom in its initial stage. Though the reign of God begins within, it works its way from the centre of human life to the circumference, and from the individual life to society in general; it is as leaven which, hidden in the meal, spreads until the whole is leavened.[2]

2. It is noteworthy that in all this teaching about the Kingdom of God mention is scarcely ever made of God as King;[3] when the King appears, it is usually Christ Himself, exercising supreme authority in His Messianic character,

[1] John iii. 3, 5 f. [2] Matt. xiii. 33.
[3] See, however, Matt. v. 35, xviii. 23, xxii. 2.

as God's Representative.[1] Of God Jesus speaks usually as Father; "My Father," "thy Father," "your Father," or simply "the Father," without indicating the person or persons to whom He stands in a paternal relation. The idea was taken over from the Old Testament; the Prophets teach the Fatherhood of God. But it is in the teaching of Christ that this view of God becomes for the first time a dominant note. In the Sermon alone, this title "Father" is used seventeen times; even in the Second Gospel it finds a place, whilst in the Fourth it meets us at every point. Moreover, on the lips of Christ it receives new meaning, and is little short of a new revelation. In the Gospels, God is not simply the Father of Israel in virtue of His covenant with the chosen people, or the Father of all men, inasmuch as they are His rational creatures, made in His image and after His likeness; the relation is at once more fundamental and more intimate. The Fatherhood of God, as it is seen in the light of the Gospel, is the counterpart of the Love of God, which embraces the world and is

[1] *E.g.*, in Matt. xxv. 34-40, xxviii. 18; John xviii. 37.

AS A WHOLE 165

not finally alienated even by its sin. No unworthiness however great, no fall however deep, no separation however long, destroys the relation; it is held in suspense, it is dormant till repentance comes, but still it exists. When the sinner turns to his Father, he finds that the Father has been waiting for him; a welcome is ready; he takes his place in the Divine household not as a servant but as a son; there is joy not only in the presence of the angels but in the fatherly Heart of God. From that hour there begins the regular exchange of paternal and filial intercourse; trust, prayer, love, service, on the one hand, and acceptance, grace, restoration of the inheritance, upon the other.[1] It is only in the sinner who repents that the paternal love of God finds free exercise, because it is only in his case that there is any capacity for understanding or reciprocating it, any response of filial feeling or performance of filial duty. But the mission of Jesus, which was the highest expression of the Divine love, was addressed to sinners without distinction;[2] and His whole

[1] Luke xv. 18 ff.   [2] Mark ii. 17; Luke xix. 10.

teaching had for its aim to bring all men to realize the Divine Fatherhood, and to claim their place in the Divine Family.

3. The relation of Jesus to the Father, and His place in the Kingdom of God, were less fully set forth in His Galilean teaching. Until the Galilean ministry was near its close, He did not even declare Himself to be the Christ; and when He did, the disciples were forbidden to make Him known in this character.[1] In contemporary Jewish thought the word suggested ideas largely alien to the purpose of His ministry; if with us it is the symbol for all that is purest and strongest in humanity, this is due to our use of "Christ." as a synonym for the personal name of our Lord. Jesus Himself, if we may judge from the Gospels, used it but rarely, and advanced personal rather than official claims. Personally, He claimed to be at once the Son of Man, representing humanity both in its weakness and its potential glory; and the Son of God, representing Deity, and fulfilling in the highest degree the filial relation to God. Both titles had their origin in the

[1] Mark viii. 30.

Old Testament—the Son of Man in Daniel's vision,[1] the Son of God in the second Psalm and in other foreshadowings of the Messianic King. But in the teaching of Jesus both acquire a new significance. They are complementary to one another, and taken together they reveal the mystery of His dual character. They proclaim Him to be a true member of the human family, and indeed its very flower and crown, and at the same time to stand in a peculiar and unique relation to God. At first sight it may seem as if when He calls God His Father the Lord claims for Himself no more than 'He attributes to every subject of the Divine Kingdom, or at most a merely official superiority. But when we examine the meaning of His Sonship, as disclosed not only in the Fourth Gospel but in some of the sayings recorded in the First and Third, it becomes evident that it differs from the sonship of believers not in degree but in kind. Jesus is the "Only Begotten," *i.e.*, the only Son ; His relation to the Father is *sui generis;* the Father is His Father in a sense in which

[1] Dan. vii. 13.

He is not and cannot be the Father of any other. His Sonship is pre-existent; it involves essential oneness with the Father; it is the basis of a perfect knowledge of the Father, it carries with it a right to all that the Father has. The author of the prologue to St. John's Gospel has surely not misread this element in our Lord's teaching when he writes, "The Word was God."

Of His mission Jesus speaks with greater freedom. Here He departs altogether from the popular conception of the Messianic *rôle*. He does not connect His work with the restoration of Jewish independence, or with His own nation or generation in any exclusive way. He was sent to humanity; if He began by evangelizing a corner of Palestine, the larger purpose was kept steadily in view. He came to be the "Light of the world," to "bear witness to the truth," to be Himself "the Truth," the Ideal in which the yearnings and hopes of the race should be realized. He came to be the life of men, saving them from sin which is death, restoring them to fellowship with God, the Source of life. To these great ends He

AS A WHOLE

directed all His thoughts and energies; He had no object in life but to fulfil the work for which He had been sent into the world. His death served the same great purpose, and served it in the highest degree. The Cross was first foretold upon the occasion when His Messianic character was first distinctly acknowledged.[1] It was not simply a foreseen consequence of His mission, but a true and essential, perhaps the most essential, factor in its fulfilment. He began by preaching the Cross as the symbol of self-sacrifice, the example which every disciple must follow in his daily life. But as the Passion approached, He proceeded to represent it as bound up in some unexplained way with the salvation of mankind. The thought had been with Him from the first; in the conversation with Nicodemus, at the first passover of the ministry, He had likened Himself to the Brazen Serpent, lifted up in the wilderness to heal serpent-bitten Israel.[2] But towards the end it was taught more openly. He must give His life, He said, a ransom for many;[3] the

[1] Mark viii. 31 ff. [2] John iii. 14.
[3] Mark x. 45.

Shepherd must die for the sheep;[1] the seed-corn must fall into the earth and die, or it would abide alone.[2] Jesus, if lifted up from the earth, would draw all men unto Him;[3] His Blood was the blood of the New Covenant, shed for many unto remission of sins.[4] The many-sidedness of this teaching will not escape the notice of the reader; there are few aspects of the Atonement which do not find an anticipation in the words of Christ. Yet He propounds no doctrine, but merely bears witness to the manifold fruits of the Passion.

Beyond His Cross and Passion the Lord foresaw not only His Resurrection and Ascension, but also His future Coming. The basis of the teaching is again supplied by a few familiar texts from the Old Testament;[5] but the application of these prophecies, the interpretation they receive, the place which they fill in Christian eschatology, are due to our Lord Himself. If the Apostolic letters and the Apocalypse have filled in the picture, the bold

[1] John x. 11. [2] John xii. 24.
[3] John xii. 32. [4] Mark xiv. 24.
[5] *E.g.*, Dan. vii. 13; Psa. cx. 1.

outline is the Master's own. Not the least remarkable feature in the teaching of Christ is this calm assurance of future triumph and glory, expressed under conditions of humiliation and mortality.

4. From the teaching of Christ as to His own person and mission we pass to His teaching in reference to the Holy Spirit. The Spirit of God appears in the Old Testament as the principle of the Divine energy manifested in creation and providence, in the endowments and work of life, in the inspiration of the prophetic order. The earlier teaching of Christ scarcely carries us beyond this view of the Spirit, except in one particular; the sphere of the Spirit's work is no longer limited to Israel, but, is regarded as co-extensive with the Kingdom of Heaven and the family of God. Our heavenly Father, we are assured, will give the Holy Spirit to them that ask Him. The gift of the Son includes the gift of the Spirit;[1] "If any man thirst," Jesus cried in the Temple, "let him come unto Me and drink.[2] All who enter the Kingdom have been born of the

---

[1] Luke xi. 13.   [2] John vii. 37.

Spirit, and the Spirit in their hearts becomes a well of water springing up into eternal life."[1] Such sayings prepare us to expect a fuller and wider manifestation of the Spirit under the New Covenant, but they do not touch the question of the Spirit's personality and relation to the Father and the Son, or the details of the Spirit's work.

These deeper teachings were reserved for the hearing of the Apostles on the night before the Passion. Then at length it became possible and necessary to speak of the dispensation which would follow the Lord's Death and Resurrection. The occasion determined the form of the revelation. The Twelve were troubled and dazed by the near approach of the Master's departure. It would take from them the Counsellor on whose guidance they had hitherto depended in every time of need. The Lord promised that He would send another Counsellor, a second Paraclete, who would recall His teaching and continue it. The term παράκλητος in this connexion was, so far as we know, entirely new; but Jesus hastens to identify the coming Paraclete with the "Holy Spirit"[2] of the

[1] John iii. 5, iv. 14.
[2] John xiv. 26, ὁ δὲ παράκλητος, τὸ πνεῦμα τὸ ἅγιον.

Psalms and the Prophets; it was the same Spirit who had inspired the Prophets and baptized the Son, by whom the work of the Son was to be carried forward and onward. The whole drift of the discourse compels us to regard the Spirit as a personal agent, distinct from the Father, distinct also from the Son, and yet in the closest relation with Both. He —the masculine pronoun is advisedly employed [1] —is to be sent by the Son from the Father, or by the Father in the Son's Name; He receives from the Son that which the Son Himself has received from the Father. He issues forth from the Father—a statement which refers no doubt to the temporal mission of the Spirit, but seems to presuppose the eternal relation which the Church teaches in the " Nicene " Creed.[2] The general effect of this teaching is to place by the side of the Father and the Son a third Divine Person, another

[1] Ἐκεῖνος (John xiv. 26, xv. 26, xvi. 8, 13 f.) refers no doubt to ὁ παράκλητος, but it carries on the suggestion of personality which that title conveys.

[2] John xv. 26, ὃ παρὰ τοῦ πατρὸς ἐκπορεύεται. The Creed uses ἐκ instead of παρά.

eternal Phase of the One Divine life—an interpretation which our Lord after His resurrection sealed with His approval when He instituted Baptism into the Name of the Three in One.

As to the operations of the Paraclete Spirit Jesus speaks with reserve; it is to the Epistles written in the light of Christian experience that we must look for a fuller pneumatology. But He marks out the great outlines of the Spirit's work after the Pentecost; His conviction of the world, His teaching of the Church, His glorifying of the Christ, His illumination of human life with the hope of the world to come.

5. From the doctrine of the Holy Spirit our thoughts pass naturally to the doctrine of the Church, in which the Spirit came to dwell. Here again the germ of the later Christian teaching is to be found in the words of Christ. The Church is mentioned in the Gospels twice only, and on both occasions in the First Gospel. In two of the Matthæan *logia* the Lord speaks of His disciples collectively as the *ecclesia*,[1] the counterpart of the "congregation" of Israel; in the first the Christian *ecclesia* is the whole body

[1] Matt. xvi. 18, xviii. 17.

AS A WHOLE 175

of believers, the ἐκκλησία καθολική of a later age; in the second the term is applied to a particular community, assembled together for worship or mutual counsel. It is interesting to note this double use of the word at its first appearance in the New Testament, in sayings attributed to our Lord Himself.

Christ regarded Himself as the Founder of a new Israel, a Divine Society upon earth. It was in His thoughts from the first, when He gathered disciples round Him, and when out of them He chose twelve and brought them into the closest association with Himself. The Twelve were in one sense the germ of the Christian ministry; in another they were the original *ecclesia*. Jesus foresaw the indefinite expansion of the Church and provided for it. This Gospel must be preached throughout the whole world, and wherever it was preached the nations would flock into the fold. To cement the union of His disciples, the Lord instituted Baptism; to maintain it, He gave the Eucharistic Food of His Body and Blood. These were among His last preparations for the new order which was to follow the Ascension. But the future of the Church had occupied His attention months before the Passion. A whole series of parables, beginning with the days of the Galilean ministry, reveals the deep interest which the subject possessed in the eyes of Christ. The Sower and the Seed, the Tares, the Mustard Seed, the Leaven, the Drag-net, the Great Supper, the Ten Virgins, are obvious examples; they describe the process of the Church's growth, its adulteration and ultimate purification, the relation of individual disciples to the body, and other kindred matters upon which ecclesiastical history has thrown a flood of light. In these parables, it is true, the Church is not mentioned by name; it is the Kingdom of Heaven which they profess to illustrate. The conclusion has been too hastily drawn that the Kingdom is identical with the Church. The two conceptions are related, but distinct; the Kingdom is the spiritual principle which the Church exhibits in a concrete form, and it transcends the Church as the spiritual transcends its visible expression. Nevertheless, the Church is no mere accident of the Divine Kingdom, but its greatest present

AS A WHOLE 177

result. A vast spiritual corporation, charged with the evangelization of the world, designed to receive all classes and races of mankind, invested with magnificent powers and assured of an indestructible vitality, is surely as splendid a conception as can be found even in the teaching of Christ. The Architect of this building of God, who laid its foundations in the obscurity of Galilee and foresaw its progress and completion, was master of the Divine art of inspiring and regenerating human life on a great scale.

6. With this vast design in His thoughts, Jesus was not less mindful of the needs of the individual. Indeed, it is with this individual spiritual life that the great bulk of His teaching is concerned. If the Third Gospel treats it with special fulness and tenderness, there is no Gospel and no part of the teaching from which it is absent. It has been said that our Lord inspired men with an " enthusiasm of humanity,"[1] and this is a true account of His own spirit, if it be understood that His zeal for the salvation of the race never led Him to over-

[1] *Ecce Homo*, c. xiv.

look the interests of individual men. The regeneration of the world to which Christ pointed was not to be attained by ignoring the needs of personal life. Nothing is more impressive in the records of His ministry than the minute care which He bestowed on those who sought His help. He did not heal or save men in the mass, but had a word for each: "Son, thy sins are forgiven";[1] "Daughter, be of good cheer; thy faith hath made thee whole."[2]

This individualism pervades His teaching. As the Physician of souls, He detected in every man a deep-seated disease which demanded separate treatment. His remedies are two—repentance and faith. Repentance is the sinner's return to his Father, with his pride broken, his delight in sin changed to aversion, his repugnance to God converted into a desire to be numbered among His servants. Faith makes the return possible, assuring the penitent of acceptance, and inspiring him with the spirit of sonship. Christ speaks of faith in God, faith in the Gospel, the message of the Love

[1] Mark. ii. 6.   [2] Matt. ix. 22.

of God, faith in Himself as the Son of God and the Saviour of men. On the last point he insists with a frequency and earnestness which shew the importance He attached to it. Trust in Jesus Christ is co-ordinated with trust in God; it includes a loyal devotion which shrinks from no sacrifice and refuses no command; it is accompanied by a love for the Master which takes the first place among the forces that move human conduct.

Each individual life, as Christ sees it, is shaping its own destinies, whether good or evil, and will receive from Him, as the Supreme Judge of men, its final award. There will be a general judgement of the race, but in this, as in the work of salvation, a full recognition will be made of the claims of the individual.

7. Our Lord's teaching with regard to future rewards and punishments calls for careful consideration.

Jesus Christ was not sent into the world to judge it, but to save it,[1] and on more than one occasion He distinctly refused the office

[1] John iii. 17.

of judge.[1] Yet His life and teaching had the effect of a judicial process, since men are judged in the sight of God according to their attitude towards the Incarnation. "He that believeth not hath been judged already; and this is the judgement, that light is come into the world, and men loved the darkness rather than the light." The remark is, perhaps, due to the Evangelist, and not to Christ, but it gives the substance of much of His teaching. This judgement is still in progress; the Church retains the sins which she is not able to remit. But the Lord also contemplates a judgement which is to come at the end of the present order, and which He connects with His return and the general resurrection of the dead. In this He will sit as Judge "in the glory of the Father with the holy angels." The manifestation of the glorified Christ will, it seems, bring to a climax the work of judgement which began with His Incarnation, and will reveal to the world and to each individual the true character of all lives.

Of the doom of the ungodly our Lord speaks

[1] Luke xii. 14; John viii. 11, 15.

AS A WHOLE 181

in terms borrowed from the popular religious teaching of His time. There is a Valley of Hinnom in the spiritual world, where the worm that feeds upon dead souls does not die, and the fire that consumes them is not quenched. The imagery is not unduly strong to depict the agony of a conscience awakened too late, of an ever-present memory of opportunities gone beyond recall. But Christ adds to these familiar descriptions; and His own words on the subject, if less realistic, are not less terrible. The unprofitable servant is cast into the outer darkness; those who have not done what they could for Christ in the person of His brethren, shall go away into eternal punishment. Whether by this expression we are to understand an absolutely interminable sentence is a question which, perhaps, does not admit of an answer. Eternity, in the sense commonly attached to the word, is an abstraction with which our Lord does not deal. He speaks of the consummation of the present αἰών, and of a new order which will take its place. A sin which passes unforgiven into that coming age is an αἰώνιον ἁμάρτημα,[1] "an eternal sin," and the punishment that will overtake it there is a κόλασις αἰώνιος,[2] "an eternal punishment." But the αἰὼν ὁ ἐρχόμενος, the future order, cannot be measured by our standards. We unconsciously transfer to it the conditions of time and space, a tendency which is apparent in modern discussions of this painful question. It is enough to know on Christ's assurance that the sentence upon the sinner involves the loss of all that the coming age holds of blessedness and hope.

"But the righteous into eternal life." So Christ paints the future of the true members of the Kingdom. The higher life of the Spirit, begun on earth, will be matured and perfected in the world to come. Here and there in His teaching the veil is partly drawn back and the life is revealed, though necessarily in terms borrowed from present experience. Men who have used their talents well shall receive more; greater endowments, larger stewardships, a wider domain, increased opportunities of

[1] Mark iii. 29.   [2] Matt. xxv. 46.

service. The principle which will guide the award is stated: "Unto every one that hath shall be given, and he shall have abundance."[1] There will be no dull uniformity of goodness or place; though all true servants enter into the joy of their Lord, they enter with powers of enjoyment varying widely according to their use of opportunities. In Christ's view there is no breach of continuity between the past and the future, between the temporal and the eternal. His judgement will but interpret and give effect to the results of human life, carrying these forward into a new order where they will serve as the ἀφορμή of the life of the world to come.

These are but faint outlines of some of the chief features in the Teaching of Christ, regarded as a whole. Our Lord did not teach systematically; His words arose out of the circumstances in which He moved, and were adapted to the intelligence of the persons whom He addressed; and this is one of the secrets of their inexhaustible

[1] Matt. xxv. 29.

charm. Yet in His teaching there are master-thoughts which dominate the whole, and bind it into a unity; and when these are brought together, it is seen to constitute a body of religious truth which has for its aim the regeneration of human life.

It is sometimes said that Christ was an eclectic, who based His teaching on ideas which already had a place in Palestinian, Alexandrian, and even Oriental thought. The theory in this form is untenable, but it may at once be conceded that our Lord deliberately built on Old Testament foundations, and availed Himself of contemporary ideas and forms of speech. It is the wisdom of a teacher to begin with the knowledge which men already possess, and to use the materials that lie in his path. But in doing this Jesus, by a spiritual alchemy, transformed into gold all that He touched. Nor did He by any means limit Himself to the work of lifting up current conceptions to a higher level, and breathing into them a new spirit. There are new things as well as old in the treasure which the Master has committed to the

AS A WHOLE 185

scribes of the Kingdom of Heaven, and the new are "things which eye saw not and ear heard not, and which entered not into the heart of man,"[1] until they were revealed by Jesus Christ. But let the teaching, whether old or new, be considered as a whole, and where can its like be found? It provides for all the spiritual needs of men, covering the whole domain of the inner life. It regulates conduct for all time by asserting principles of universal application. It fixes the highest standards, and at the same time supplies the strongest motives for endeavouring to reach them. "Love your enemies," it commands, adding, "that ye may be sons of your Father which is in heaven:" "ye shall be perfect, as your heavenly Father is perfect."[2]

If it be objected that an attempt to reconstruct society on lines such as these is chimerical, and as a matter of fact has never been realized, the answer is that the character which Christ sets before men, and which He Himself exhibited, is one which with us can

[1] Cor. ii. 9. [2] Matt. v. 4 f., 48.

have only its beginnings in the present world. He lived and would have men live for the eternal and the infinite. The Kingdom of Heaven within us must ever be an ideal which is above our present efforts, pointing us on to another state where it will have its perfect work. Meanwhile it is not inoperative or destitute of results. If the world has not yet been transfigured by the teaching of our Lord, no other teaching has done so much to make its crooked ways straight and its rough places plain. If the religion of Jesus Christ has not yet produced a perfect saint, it has planted in the lives of tens of thousands a principle which makes for perfection, and will attain it, as our faith assures us, in the day of the Lord's Return.

οὐδέποτε ἐλάλησεν οὕτως ἄνθρωπος.
                      St. John vii. 46.

www.ingramcontent.com/pod-product-compliance
Lightning Source LLC
Chambersburg PA
CBHW050805160426
43192CB00010B/1647